Hi. My name is Ed, and I have ALS (Lou Gehrig's disease or motor neuron disease). I thought that if I ever got a terminal disease, it would force me to pray and read the Bible more. When I was diagnosed, I found the opposite to be true: I could barely pray or read the Bible. It took every ounce of energy I had to get out of bed and face another day. These prayers and reflections are for those who feel the same way. I have included a short prayer for every morning and a devotional for every evening. These prayers and devotionals have helped me cultivate hope in the midst of the darkness of this disease. I pray that they will do the same for you.

Note: Ed Dobson passed away in 2015, fifteen years beyond his ALS diagnosis. His courageous faith and transcendent strength infuse these prayers and devotions with meaning and hope.

Prayers & Promises

*when facing a
life-threatening illness*

Prayers & Promises

when facing a
life-threatening illness

30 Short
Morning
and
Evening
Reflections

Ed Dobson

ZONDERVAN®

ZONDERVAN

Prayers and Promises When Facing a Life-Threatening Illness
© 2007 by Edward G. Dobson

Requests for information should be addressed to:
Zondervan, 3900 Sparks Dr. SE, Grand Rapids, Michigan 49546

ISBN 978-0-310-27612-8 (audiobook)
ISBN 978-0-310-46303-0 (TP)

Library of Congress Cataloging-in-Publication Data

Dobson, Ed.
    Prayers and promises when facing a life threatening illness : 30 short
morning and evening reflections / Ed Dobson.
        p. cm.
    ISBN-10: 0-310-27427-3 (hardcover)
    ISBN-13: 978-0-310-27427-8 (hardcover)
    1. Terminally ill — Prayer-books and devotions — English. 2. Terminally
ill — Religious life. I. Title.
BV4910.D56 2007
242'.4 — dc22

                                                                2006034923

Interior design by Michelle Espinoza

Contents

Introduction from a Fellow Pilgrim

I first noticed a problem when I was backpacking. I had difficulty opening jars and bottles. I thought, *Well, you just turned fifty, and this is what happens when you get old.* Then I started getting twitches in my back and in my arm muscles. My wife encouraged me to see a doctor. But being typically male, I blew off her advice. One day I was writing out my sermon notes, and I had this strange feeling—as if my mind and my hand were not cooperating. My hand seemed to be a few seconds behind my brain. This frightened me.

The next Sunday morning, I was in church, sitting on the front row. Seated behind me was a friend who is a neurologist. During the congregational singing before the sermon, I turned to him and said, "I have been having this weakness in my hands, and lately my muscles have been twitching. When I was writing out my sermon notes, I had this strange sensation that my brain and my hand were not coordinated. What do you think?" Of course, a physician is not going to give a diagnosis during the singing prior to the sermon. "I think you'd better come and see me," he said. "Like tomorrow morning."

So I went to see the neurologist the next day. After examining me and testing my muscle strength, he sat me down in his office. "There is a continuum of possibilities," he said. "You may have benign fasciculations. Everyone has twitches in their muscles. Maybe you have more twitches than the average person. On the other hand, you may have motor neuron disease—known as ALS or Lou Gehrig's disease." When the doctor mentioned ALS (amyotrophic lateral sclerosis), I was completely stunned. Several people in our church had died of ALS. One of them was a young man who lived for seven years after he was diagnosed. I had visited him about once a month for those seven years and preached his funeral. Another was an older man who lived for eleven months after he was diagnosed.

My neurologist referred me to the University of Michigan ALS clinic for further testing. A few weeks later the doctors confirmed that I had a motor neuron disease and that it was most likely ALS, a degenerative, incurable, and terminal disease. They gave me a large folder filled with information about my disease and basically told me that there was nothing they could do for me except to help me manage my increasing disability. They told me that there is no known cause for this disease and no known cure. They said that I would have two to five years to live, and that most of that time would be in a disabled condition.

When you are told you have an incurable and terminal disease, no words can describe the sinking feeling you have. Outside Jerusalem, beyond the Mount of Olives, there is a place called Bethany, the ancient home of Mary, Martha, and Lazarus. Up one of the back alleys is a Second Temple period tomb. Outside the tomb a sign indicates, "The Tomb of Lazarus." After paying a modest entrance fee, visitors descend a long spiral staircase. Down and down and down. When they reach the bottom, they crawl under a large stone, and on the other side they see a burial chamber. It is far from the warmth of the sunshine on the street, dark, confining, and claustrophobic. This is what a terminal disease feels like. You descend from the warmth and sunshine into a dark and confining space. You descend into the tomb of Lazarus, and you think that you will never return to the sunshine.

So when you find it difficult to read the Bible or even pray, what do you do? How do you climb out of the tomb of Lazarus? After my illness was diagnosed, I discovered that my ability to focus on God, the Bible, and prayer was significantly limited. I could take spiritual truth only in small bites. Over the next several months, God inspired me to forge some simple prayers that helped me climb out of the tomb of Lazarus. Some days I walk in the warmth and sunshine of hope. On other days I am in the darkness of the tomb of Lazarus. Every day is a struggle, and every day I must do all I can to keep climbing the staircase out of the tomb.

I offer these prayers and promises as a guide for those who face a life-threatening illness and for those who care for them. I am still very much on the journey. I do not have all of the answers. But I have discovered the power of these simple prayers and promises to help me along the way. I encourage you to pray one of these prayers each day. After you have completed the thirty-day cycle, do it again. After each selection, space is provided for you to write down your own comments or journal notes.

A fellow pilgrim,
Ed Dobson

Day One

Morning Prayer

God, help me to live for today and to enjoy it to its fullest.

We know that every day is a gift from God, but we often take that gift for granted. Having a life-threatening or terminal disease is a constant reminder that your days are numbered. All human beings know their days are numbered, but very few ever give it any thought. Most people live every day as if they had an unlimited number of days ahead of them. Having a life-threatening or terminal disease changes all of that. Every day that passes is one day closer to the end.

One of the problems of having a terminal disease is the tendency to live in the future and not the present. And living in the future is a guarantee of depression. Whenever I spend too much time thinking about the future and what it holds for me, I begin to sink deep into despair. The issues facing me in the future are not very pleasant. What about a wheelchair? What about breathing assistance? What about swallowing? What about a feeding tube? And the list goes on. Everybody I know who has a terminal disease is faced with similar issues. I'm not afraid of being dead. I'm afraid of getting dead.

Over the years, I have had a very close relationship with several African-American pastors in our community. We have eaten together, played golf together, laughed together, traveled together, and cried together. We have spent hundreds of hours together. In the process we have become close friends. I noticed early on in our relationship that African-American pastors pray differently than white pastors do. Their prayers emerge out of a long history of suffering, and for that reason, they are a lot different than white prayers. African-American pastors almost always begin their prayers this way: "God, thank you for waking me up this morning." I don't think I have ever heard a white pastor pray such a prayer. We take waking up for granted. But those who suffer do not take waking up for granted. They are grateful for every day that God gives them. And they recognize the goodness of God with the rising sun.

So this day I pray, "God, thank you for waking me up this morning." I want to embrace every day, however limited my days may be, as a gift from God. I want to live this day to its fullest. I know there are things I can no longer do. I know I am facing daily limitations. But I want to focus on what I can do, not on what I cannot do. "So help me God. I know this day will never be repeated. I know I cannot live it over again. Help me to live it to its fullest."

Evening Promise
God is pursuing you.

The Lord God called to the man, "Where are you?"
(Genesis 3:9)

The Bible begins with a powerful statement: "In the beginning God created the heavens and the earth." Following this statement we have the unfolding story of creation. However one reads this story, one thing is clear: God did it! He spoke and it was done.

On the sixth day, God created Adam. "So God created man in his own image, in the image of God he created him; male and female he created them" (Genesis 1:27). First, "the LORD God formed the man from the dust of the ground and breathed into his nostrils the breath of life, and the man became a living being" (2:7). When he saw that it was not good for the man to be alone, he made Eve from one of Adam's ribs (2:18–23).

God then placed Adam and Eve in the garden to take care of it. They were free to eat from all of the trees of the garden except for the Tree of Knowledge of Good and Evil. God warned them that if they ate of that tree they would surely die. You know the story. Adam and Eve listened to the serpent. They chose to disobey God and ate the forbidden fruit. And as soon as they did, "the eyes of both of them were opened, and they realized they were naked; so they sewed fig leaves together and make coverings for themselves" (Genesis 3:7). Paradise had been shattered. Sin had entered into the world. Adam and Eve had chosen to disregard the word of God.

So if you were God, what would you have done? Would you have killed Adam and Eve right there? After all, you promised that if they ate of the fruit, they would immediately die. God, nevertheless, did not kill them right then. Instead, he came walking in the garden in "the cool of the day" (Genesis 3:8). He called to Adam, "Where are you?" *Where are you?* — what a question. Didn't God know where Adam and Eve were? Of course he did; he's God. Then why did he ask the question? He asked the question because he wanted Adam and Eve to know that he cared. He wanted them to know that he was pursuing them.

This is God's motif throughout the entire Bible. The Bible is not the story of us human beings pursuing God. Rather, it is the story of God pursuing us. God called Abraham and Moses. God gave the Torah on Mount Sinai. God expressed his love by sending his Son, Jesus, into the world. God sent the Holy Spirit after Jesus ascended to heaven. Yes, the Bible is the story of God pursuing us.

So even though I feel abandoned by God, even though my prayers seem to get no further than the ceiling in my bedroom, even though I feel lost, one abiding truth remains: God has not abandoned me. God is not silent. God is pursuing me and asking, "Where are you?" God cares about my condition and is moving in the circumstances of my life, as broken as they may be. He cares where I am at.

So be encouraged. The God who came down from heaven to pursue Adam and Eve is the same God who comes into your life and cares about you. He is still asking the same question: "Where are you?" So answer him: "I'm here God. I'm struggling. I'm sinking. I'm in darkness. I'm afraid. But thanks for asking."

Day Two

Morning Prayer
God, help me to realize that it's not over until it's over.

At Christmastime, a few months after my diagnosis, we were doing our annual Christmas program at the church. This program is a major outreach into our community. We encourage our people to bring their friends and neighbors with them. During the program, I take about ten minutes to share the good news of the gospel and the real meaning of Christmas. Over the years, many people have come to know Christ in a personal way through our Christmas program. But this year I did not feel like going. I did not feel like speaking. I did not feel like sharing the gospel. I did not want to be around people. I wanted to sit home alone and avoid all of the questions that people would ask me.

But my wife said, "You need to go. There are people who need to hear the gospel. You need to be there." So I reluctantly got in my truck and began driving to the church. I had barely gone a mile when my cell phone rang. It was Billy Schneider. Billy and I had been friends for years. He had been a heroin addict for more than twenty years in New York City. Then he came to know the Lord, and God radically changed his life. He had just finished a bout with cancer, and he also is HIV positive. He has more things wrong in his body than most people, yet he is still alive. He called to encourage me.

At first I was mad that I had answered the cell phone. I really didn't want to talk to anybody. But now I was stuck. Billy told me, "You need to be a Yogi Berra Christian." I thought, *What in the world does that mean? What does it mean to be a Yogi Berra Christian?* I thought that maybe since Yogi had something to do with the New York Yankees and my disease was named after Lou Gehrig, there was some connection. When I asked Billy what he meant, I found out I was wrong. He quoted one of Yogi Berra's famous sayings: "It ain't over till it's over." Billy then said, "You need to be a Yogi Berra Christian. Remember it ain't over till it's over."

That was exactly what I needed to hear. I was beginning to believe and accept that my life was in fact over. As I drove to church that night, I had been thinking that this might be my last Christmas to speak at the Christmas program. That this might be my last winter to see the snow. That this might be my last Christmas with the family. For me, it was almost over. Then Billy reminded me of Yogi Berra. Then I prayed, "God, help me to realize that it ain't over till it's over."

One day it will be over. One day I will leave this life and enter into eternity with Christ. And so will you. And so will everyone else. But I don't want to rush my entrance into the kingdom. The fact that you are reading these devotions means that your earthly life isn't over. So stop acting as if it is.

Evening Promise

God will provide, but sometimes he comes through
at the last minute.

"God himself will provide the lamb for the burnt offering, my son."
(Genesis 22:8)

God spoke to Abraham and said, "*Lech lecha*" (Hebrew for "Go forth"). Abraham left his country, his people, and his father's house at the Lord's command, and God promised Abraham that his descendants would be a great nation and that all the peoples on earth would be blessed through him. All this sounded good, but there was a fundamental problem: Abraham and Sarah were old and had no children. Nevertheless, God kept his word, and in their old age, they gave birth to a son named Isaac. He was the child of promise.

Sometime later God tested Abraham. He said, "Take your son, your only son, Isaac, whom you love, and go to the region of Moriah. Sacrifice him there as a burnt offering on one of the mountains I will tell you about" (Genesis 22:2). Child sacrifice was deeply embedded in the culture of Abraham's day. Whenever there was a crisis in the tribe or village, the priest would designate a person as a human sacrifice. In this way they hoped to appease the gods. Perhaps Abraham assumed that his God was like the other gods of the land and now wanted a human sacrifice. Whatever Abraham was thinking, this had to be an incredible test. Isaac was his only son. He was clearly the key to the future. And now God was asking Abraham to sacrifice the key to the future.

So Abraham and Isaac made their way up the mountain to perform this terrible act. When Isaac asked about a lamb for the burnt offering, Abraham answered, "God himself will provide the lamb for the burnt offering, my son." As they made their way up one side of the mountain in pain and uncertainty, the ram was making its way up the other side of the mountain. At the last moment, when Abraham was about to kill his son, God stopped him and provided the lamb. Some of the ancient rabbis contended that the ram came all the way from the garden of Eden. On the long journey it was delayed and made it there just in time.

This story holds a powerful lesson. As I make my way up the mountain of disease knowing that every step is a struggle, God is already providing a lamb that is coming up the other side of the mountain. And at the right time, in the providence of God, we will meet. I cannot see it, but I know it is there. Do I now have the grace to face another bad report from the doctor? No! Do I need the grace to face another bad report from the doctor? Yes! So where is that grace? The ram is already coming up the other side of the mountain. Do I now have the grace to face the process of dying? No! Do I need the grace to face the process of dying? Yes! So where is that grace? The ram is already coming up the other side of the mountain. God's grace is already on the way. And he will provide that grace at the right moment even if it is the last moment.

Day 3

Morning Prayer
God, help me not to worry.

We know that we are not supposed to worry. Jesus himself made that clear. "Therefore I tell you, do not worry about your life, what you will eat or drink; or about your body, what you will wear. Is not life more important than food, and the body more important than clothes?" (Matthew 6:25). But I am worried about eating and drinking. One of the challenges of my disease is that eventually my swallowing muscles will be affected, making it difficult for me to swallow. Then I will have to make a choice about a feeding tube put directly into my stomach. So I am worried about eating and drinking. I am not worried about what I will eat or drink, but I am worried about the very acts of eating and drinking. So when Jesus tells me not to worry, this is a problem.

I have friends who tell me not to worry. Whenever I express my concerns about the future, they say, "Hey man, don't worry. God will take care of you." That's easy for them to say; they don't have a terminal disease. They don't have the prospect of increasing disability. They are not facing death and dying. It is easy to believe that God will take care of you when you don't need to be taken care of. But when you desperately need the care of God for the ultimate issues of life, it is not so easy to stop worrying.

But Jesus does offer us hope. He goes on to say in Matthew 6: "Look at the birds of the air; they do not sow or reap or store away in barns, and yet your heavenly Father feeds them. Are you not much more valuable than they?" (v. 26). The God who is vitally interested in birds and their survival is vitally interested in me and my survival. And the God who takes care of and feeds the birds will take care of and feed me.

Look out your window and find a bird. God knows that bird. God sees that bird. God feeds that bird. God takes care of that bird. Jesus reminds us that we are much more valuable than birds. God knows us. God sees us. God feeds us. God takes care of us. So I have learned to pray, "God, help me not to worry. I know you love me. I know you see me. And I know that you will take care of me." And every time I see a bird, I am reminded of that promise. Fortunately, I live at a place where there are a lot of birds.

Evening Promise
I will not be afraid.

God has said,

"Never will I leave you;
never will I forsake you."

So we say with confidence,

"The Lord is my helper; I will not be afraid.
What can man do to me?"

(Hebrews 13:5–6)

Hebrews 13:5–6 has helped me in my struggle with ALS more than any other passage in the entire Bible. I especially like the phrase "I will not be afraid." Fear is a paralyzing force in our lives. It is especially paralyzing when you have a life-threatening or terminal disease. I am not afraid of being dead. After all, I know where I'm going. When I die I will be "absent from the body and present with the Lord" (see 1 Corinthians 5:8). But I am afraid of getting dead. The process of dying is scary.

Having read extensively of literature on ALS, I am fully aware of all that I face in the future. And it is not a pleasant prospect. In my particular case, the neurons in the nerves die, and the electrical impulse from the brain to the muscle stops functioning. When this happens the muscle quits working and eventually atrophies. Currently I have the disease in my hands, arms, chest, back, and tongue. According to the prognosis, the disease will continue to spread. People in the advanced stages of this disease are wheelchair-bound and have difficulty breathing and swallowing. Eventually it kills them. Meanwhile, throughout the entire process the brain works fine.

The more I think about the future, the more afraid I become. Some would say I have a lack of faith. I'm not sure if I do have a lack of faith. I'm simply telling you, "I'm afraid!" Soon after my diagnosis, I learned to take five-minute time-outs. Whenever fear would begin taking over my life, I would take a time-out and repeat the verses from Hebrews 13: "God has said, 'Never will I leave you; never will I forsake you.' So we say with confidence, 'The Lord is my helper; I will not be afraid.'" I would say these words over and over for the entire five minutes. The first time through I was reciting words, but I really didn't believe their truth. It was only as I repeated them over and over that I actually began to believe them.

I know what the doctors say about my disease, and I know what my prognosis is, but I really don't know what the future holds. I do, however, know the One who has the future in his control: God. And he has promised that he will never leave me nor forsake me. He has promised to be my helper. Whatever I face, he will be there. If I need to make a decision about a wheelchair, he will be there to help me. If I have to make a decision about a feeding tube, he will be there to help me. If I have to make a decision about breathing assistance, he will be there to help me. And when I come to the end of my earthly journey, he will be there to help me. So I keep telling myself, "I will not be afraid!"

I wrote these verses on a three-by-five card and placed the card on the mirror by my bed. They are the first words I look at every morning when I get up, and they are the last words I look at when I go to bed. When my youngest son went off to war in Iraq with the Army National Guard, I gave him one of the cards that was on the mirror by my bed. I wanted him to know that in the face of fear, God would be with him.

Day 4

Morning Prayer
God, I surrender myself and my future completely to you.

Every day my life is characterized by a battle for who is in control. When I take control of my life, I tend to get in trouble. I also tend to get depressed because there is nothing I can do for my disease. Still I'd like to be in control. But, in reality, control is only an illusion. No one is in control of his life or his future. So it would make logical sense to surrender control of our lives and futures to God. Right? The problem is that it is much easier to talk about surrender than it is to actually surrender.

After my diagnosis I was preaching a series of messages on stewardship. In the middle of the sermon, I got this crazy idea. I was talking about the church at Corinth who first gave themselves to the Lord. So I asked one of the ushers to bring me an offering plate. Then I told the congregation that when the ushers passed the plates for the offering, everyone should have placed the plate on the floor and stood in it. So I put the offering plate on the floor and stood in it and preached the rest of my sermon in the offering plate. At the end of the sermon, I asked, "What part of your life is not in the plate? What are you holding back from God?"

After the third service, I was walking down the back hallway and asking myself the same question, "What part of your life is not in the plate? What are you holding back from God?"

As I was walking down the back steps, I became aware that my tongue was not in the offering plate. I had dealt with the issue of not being able to use my arms or legs, but I had not dealt with the issue of speaking. I was holding back my tongue from God. So I told God, "I give you my tongue. I give you my speaking. If this is the last sermon I ever preach, it's okay with me." This was the first time since my diagnosis that I totally and completely surrendered everything to God.

Some people in our congregation got a video of the sermon. They then made a photograph from the video of me standing in the plate. At the bottom of the photograph they put some words that my dad had given me: "You are indispensable until your work on earth is done." I have that photograph in my office as a constant reminder that my life is in God's hands and that I am to be living my life in the plate. One of my problems is that I keep getting out of the plate. So I have to constantly pray, "God, I surrender myself and my future completely to you."

Evening Promise
Faith is not the absence of doubt.

"Everything is possible for him who believes." (Mark 9:23)

On one occasion a man with a demon-possessed son brought that son to the disciples to get him help. The son had a serious problem. His father reported, "He foams at the mouth, gnashes his teeth and becomes rigid" (Mark 9:18). Watching your children suffer is much more difficult than suffering yourself. I would much prefer that I have my disease than any of my children having it. This father must have felt the same way, so he brought his son to Jesus' disciples. Nevertheless, they were unable to help him.

Then the man brought his son to Jesus. The evil spirit immediately threw the boy on the ground, and he began foaming at the mouth. Jesus asked the dad how long the son had been like this. The father replied, "From childhood.... It has often thrown him into the fire or water to kill him. But if you can do anything, take pity on us and help us" (vv. 21–22). Jesus responded, "'If you can?'... Everything is possible for him who believes" (v. 23). In the Gospels, when Jesus heals, he appeals to the issue of faith. His answer to this dad was a common answer: If you believe, all things are possible.

The father responded with one of the most remarkable and honest statements in the Gospels: "I do believe; help me overcome my unbelief!" (v. 24). He admitted that he had both faith and doubt. I often see "faith healers" on religious television who believe that when Jesus died on the cross, he not only died to save us, but also to heal us. They believe that everybody can be healed but that a person's healing is entirely a matter of faith. If a person has enough faith, he or she can be healed. If a person is not healed, it is because of a lack of faith. This puts an incredible amount of pressure on the one who is sick. It means that if I have enough faith, I will be healed, but if I do not have enough faith, I will not be healed.

The truth is that I have faith to believe God can heal me. But the truth is also that I have a lot of doubts. Sometimes my faith overcomes my doubt, and at other times doubt overcomes my faith. My life is a mixture of both. That's why I love the story of this man. He was honest enough to admit to Jesus that he had both faith and doubt. Jesus did not say, "Come back when you have enough faith." He did not say, "Get rid of the doubt, and then I can help you." No! Jesus rebuked the evil spirit and healed the boy.

The disciples of course were bothered by this. They wanted to know why they couldn't drive out the evil spirit. Jesus said, "This kind can come out only by prayer" (v. 29). Jesus was reminding them that the power to overcome Satan comes through prayer. So I learned two things from this story. First, faith is not the absence of doubt. I can believe God for healing and doubt him for a healing at the same time. And the presence of doubt does not eliminate the possibility of a miracle. Second, the ultimate issue is prayer. Even when I have doubt and questions, I can still pray. And prayer opens up the possibility of a miracle from God. So when I'm watching television and a religious leader tells me that my miracle is dependent on my faith, I go back to this story of the man with a demon-possessed son. My miracle is ultimately up to God—it is not up to me. And what God does, he does in answer to prayer.

Day 5

Morning Prayer
God, thank you for waking me up this morning.

Over the years, I have developed some wonderful relationships with African-American pastors in our community. They are my closest friends in ministry. We have worshiped and worked together and laughed and cried together. I have learned much about God and the Bible from them. One of the first things I learned was that African-American pastors pray differently than white pastors. They often begin their prayers this way: "Dear God, thank you for waking me up this morning."

I do not recall any white pastor ever praying a prayer like this. The African-American community has a long history of suffering and struggle. They read the Bible as an oppressed minority, and their suffering has influenced the way they pray. They are grateful for every day God gives them, and they take nothing for granted. They recognize that their only hope for survival is God. So they pray, "Dear God, thank you for waking me up this morning."

Like my African-American brothers, I am also in the midst of a struggle—a struggle with a terminal disease. So I am learning to be grateful for every day God gives me. I cannot relive the past, and the future looks rather bleak, so I focus on today. And I recognize that this day is a gift from God. I may not be in the best of health, and I may not be able to do all of the things I used to do, but I am here and I am alive. This is a gift from God.

So I am learning to begin every day with this simple prayer: "Dear God, thank you for waking me up this morning."

Evening Promise
Sometimes I feel like the rock.

"Walk on ahead of the people. Take with you some of the elders of Israel and take in your hand the staff with which you struck the Nile, and go. I will stand there before you by the rock at Horeb. Strike the rock, and water will come out of it for the people to drink." (Exodus 17:5–6)

The desert is a difficult place to live. Several years ago I hiked from Jericho up to Jerusalem in the Wadi Kelt during the month of July, which is one of the hottest times of the year. It was well over 100 degrees in the shade. We hiked all day long. Toward the end of the hike, several of the people in our group sat down and began to cry uncontrollably. They said, "I can't go any farther. I cannot take another step." I felt the same way. It took every ounce of strength I had to put one foot in front of the other and take the next step.

After the children of Israel were delivered from Egypt, they wandered in the desert. Soon they were both hungry and thirsty. To meet their needs, God first provided manna. The manna appeared on the ground every morning, and the people collected enough for that day. On the sixth day they were to collect enough for the sixth day and for the Sabbath. God provided for them on a daily basis. Second, God provided water. The people began complaining because of their lack of water (Exodus 17:1–3), so God gave Moses an instruction. "Walk on ahead of the people. Take with you some of the elders of Israel and take in your hand thes staff with which you struck the Nile, and go. I will stand there before you by the rock at Horeb. Strike the rock, and water will come out of it for the people to drink." Water did come out of the rock, and the people were satisfied.

We learn from this story that God provides food and water in the desert. Similarly, when you have a serious illness, you are in the desert. Every step is demanding. Sometimes you feel like sitting down and crying and saying to God, "I cannot go one step further." You are hungry and thirsty, and God always provides just enough to get you through that day.

As I read this story, however, I feel like I have much in common with the rock. A rock does not produce water. It can't. It's a rock. The makeup of a rock is not conducive to producing anything. It's too hard. That is how I feel with the disease I have. I feel hard. I feel immovable. I feel stuck. But in the desert God performed an amazing miracle: he brought water from the rock. He did the impossible. And I know God can do that in my life as well. When I feel like I'm hard and stuck, God can produce water from the rock. He can do the impossible in my life.

Disease is no obstacle to God. From a human and medical point of view, it may be a rock. But God can bring water from the rock. Water represents life. Without it the children of Israel would have died in the desert. Without water I would have died on the long hike from Jericho to Jerusalem. And without God's help now I can't make it another day. But he brings water from the rock and gives me hope and life for another day. When I feel like a rock, I'm encouraged. I know God can do the impossible with a rock. So I'm asking God to do the impossible in my life today: "God, bring water out of the rock. Give me life and hope and strength for this day."

Day 6

Morning Prayer

God, give me the grace to let go of my family.

When you are diagnosed with a terminal disease, one of the first questions that comes to mind is, what about my family? Shortly after I was diagnosed, our first grandchild was born. The day she was born, I went with my wife to see the baby. I took Lucy in my arms and dedicated her to the Lord. As I prayed, I wondered if I would ever see her grow up. Would I see her go to kindergarten? Would I see her graduate from high school? Would I see her go to college? Would I see her fall in love and get married? As I stood there holding Lucy in my arms, I had a deep aching in my heart. I knew that the answers to these questions would probably be no.

Leaving behind your children, your spouse, and your grandchildren is no easy task. On the outside you try to act like everything is fine. You smile and laugh and interact with them as you always have. But deep inside you constantly worry about your future and their future. You think, *I just want to see them grow up. I just want to be there with them.* The thought of leaving them behind is far more pressing and difficult than the thought of dealing with your own disease and death. So I have learned to pray, "God, give me the grace to let go of my family."

The truth is that God will take care of my family. The truth is that in God's hands they are better off than they would be if they were in my hands. The truth is that God will sustain and guide them without my being there. And so my prayer is not for them. God will take care of them. My prayer is for me. I need the grace to let them go. So I am learning to place my family in God's hands every day. Whenever I do that, I have a deep peace about the future. But whenever I begin to feel that my family needs me and that I need them, I get very depressed and emotional. At that point I am retaking control of my family. So I have to re-surrender them to God, asking God again for the grace to let them go. Sometimes I have to pray this prayer several times a day: "God, give me the grace to let go of my family."

Evening Promise
Don't worry.

"Therefore do not worry about tomorrow, for tomorrow will worry about itself. Each day has enough trouble of its own."
(Matthew 6:34)

Jesus tells us in his Sermon on the Mount not to worry. That's easy to say, but it's very difficult to put into practice. I don't worry at all about the past. The past is the past, and there is nothing I can do to change it. But I do worry about the future. And that is how Jesus begins his instruction about worry—by talking about the cares of the future. "Do not worry about your life, what you will eat or drink; or about your body, what you will wear. Is not life more important than food, and the body more important than clothes?" (Matthew 6:25). Notice his use of the future tense—"what you will eat or drink ... what you will wear." Jesus knows that our greatest tendency is to worry about the future.

I worry most about the future. What will I do when I can no longer walk? What will I do if I am in a wheelchair and I have to adapt the house to accommodate the wheelchair? Who will take care of my wife when I'm gone? Who will look out for the kids when I'm gone? Questions. Questions. Questions. The list goes on and on. There is never a shortage of issues to worry about. I often feel like David.

> *My heart is in anguish within me;*
> *   the terrors of death assail me.*
> *Fear and trembling have beset me;*
> *   horror has overwhelmed me.*
> *I said, "Oh, that I had the wings of a dove!*
> *   I would fly away and be at rest —*
> *I would flee far away*
> *   and stay in the desert;*
> *I would hurry to my place of shelter,*
> *   far from the tempest and storm." (Psalm 55:4–8)*

I often sit on my porch watching the birds through the window. As I watch them, I wish that I had wings and could fly away far from my troubles and disease. *If I could just exchange places with one of those birds,* I think. *Then life would be okay!* Then I remember Jesus' words dealing with worry from his Sermon on the Mount: "Look at the birds of the air; they do not sow or reap or store away in barns, and yet your heavenly Father feeds them. Are you not much more valuable than they? Who of you by worrying can add a single hour to his life?" (Matthew 6:26–27). This passage reminds me when I feel like flying away like a bird that God takes care of the birds. God knows each bird, cares for each bird, and knows when each bird dies. If God does that for birds, will he not much more take care of me?

So what is my responsibility in regard to not worrying? Jesus tells us. "Seek first his kingdom and his righteousness, and all these things will be given to you as well" (Matthew 6:33). When I put God first in everything I do, he takes care of all of the details of life. So the next time you see a bird, remember that God takes care of that bird and God will take care of you. Also remember that it is your responsibility to seek God first.

Day 7

Morning Prayer
God, give me the grace to let go of my job.

For the last nineteen years I have been the senior pastor of Calvary Church in Grand Rapids, Michigan. I have loved every minute of my ministry in Grand Rapids. I love to preach. I love to lead. I love to evangelize. I love to meet with people. I love to visit the hospitals. I love to do funerals and weddings. I love committee and board meetings. This is what I was called to do, and this is what I love doing. While I have experienced challenges, difficulties, and failures, I still cannot think of doing anything else other than pastoring. And I cannot think of another place I would rather do it than at Calvary Church in Grand Rapids. I am trying to tell you that I love being a pastor.

Resigning from Calvary Church was one of the most difficult things I have ever done. It took me several years to get up the courage to do it. Since my diagnosis the church has been especially kind to me. They allowed me to adjust my schedule and to reduce the number of times I preached each week. They helped reorganize the church so I would not be responsible for all of the administrative and day-to-day ministries. But I soon realized that even though my schedule had been adjusted and my workload had been reduced, I could no longer fulfill all the duties of being the senior pastor. So I had to face the reality that the church needed someone else to be the senior pastor.

I am indebted to the head of the ALS clinic at the University of Michigan for her advice. She told me that the best thing I could do for my disease was to step away from the responsibilities of being the pastor at Calvary Church. So when I returned from my annual visit, I informed the board that I would be stepping down as pastor of Calvary Church. I decided that I would make a total break with the church. I would not stay on during the transition. I would not attend the church. For my health and for the health of the church, I felt that a complete separation was important.

Letting go of what I was called to do was immensely difficult. This was the only life I had known for nineteen years. This was the only place I had served for nineteen years. I knew the people, the culture, the community, and the church. Now I was leaving all of that behind for a very uncertain future. So I constantly prayed, "God, give me the grace to let go of my job." And God answered my prayers. After my last service on a Sunday, I walked up the steps of the platform and out the back door with my family. I got in the car and drove out of the parking lot for the last time. And as I drove out the back driveway, I had this overwhelming sense of relief. I was no longer responsible for the church. All of the pressure had been alleviated. I was free.

Many months have passed since that night. Although I desperately miss all of the people at Calvary Church, I know I did the right thing. And I know that God has given me grace to move beyond my ministry there.

Letting go of our jobs is difficult for those of us who have a tendency to base our self-worth on what we do, because leaving our jobs has a profound impact on our self-worth. But God's grace is sufficient for even that. So learn to pray, "God, give me the grace to let go of my job. And give me the grace to see my identity as more than what I do."

Evening Promise
I've been reduced to a stump.

A shoot will come up from the stump of Jesse;
from his roots a Branch will bear fruit.
The Spirit of the LORD will rest on him. (Isaiah 11:1 – 2)

Isaiah gives a twofold prophecy. First, the line of Jesse will be cut off as one cuts the branches from a tree and reduces it to a stump. Second, from this stump a new branch will emerge, and that branch is the promised Messiah. The Spirit of the Lord will rest on him. When the inhabitants of Jerusalem went into Babylonian captivity in 586 BC, the line of David (the descendants of Jesse) were cut off. Even though they returned from captivity and rebuilt Jerusalem and the temple, the monarchy had come to an end. The tree had been reduced to a stump.

I know the feeling. With one visit to the doctor I had been reduced to a stump. It was as if all my branches had been cut off. My hopes and dreams for the future had been cut off. The prospects of seeing my children and grandchildren grow up had been cut off. The prospects of preaching and serving God in pastoral ministry for another fifteen years had been cut off. I had been reduced to a stump. And being this stump is not much fun.

However, the prophet predicts that a new branch will emerge from this stump and bear fruit. This is a reference to the coming Messiah — Jesus Christ.

The Spirit of the LORD will rest on him —
the Spirit of wisdom and of understanding,
the Spirit of counsel and of power,

the Spirit of knowledge and of the fear of the LORD—
and he will delight in the fear of the LORD. (Isaiah 11:2–3)

God can take a stump and out of that stump produce something greater than what was there before. The line of David was cut off, but out of that stump, God sent his one and only Son into the world as a descendant of David.

This is my hope as well. When I have been reduced to a stump, I can trust in God who is able to cause branches to grow out of this stump. When the Israelites were taken into captivity and the line of David was cut off, it was a dark day in Jewish history. Although they later returned, things were never quite the same. But God had an even better future for them than they could have imagined. And the same is true for me. Even though I am facing a debilitating and terminal disease, I know God has a wonderful future for me. And that future is not just in heaven. It is right here and now. So I ask for a spirit of wisdom, understanding, counsel, power, and knowledge.

Morning Prayer

God, give me courage to ask forgiveness
of the people I have offended over the years.

Shortly after I was diagnosed, I decided that since I was going to die, I wanted to die with a clear conscience. I knew I had offended people over the years with what I had said or done, so I made a list of all the people I had offended. I made the decision that I would call or talk to each of them and ask forgiveness. For me this was difficult. I knew that in some cases I was right from a biblical point of view and the persons I had offended were wrong. I knew they would interpret my asking forgiveness as their being right and my being wrong. I knew they would go to their circle of friends and inform them that I was completely wrong and that I had asked for forgiveness. Nevertheless, I finally decided that the right thing to do was to seek forgiveness. Whatever they did with that forgiveness was up to them and not to me.

And so I began calling and meeting with people. The whole experience was liberating. I knew that I could die with a clear conscience. I also made a list of all the staff people who had either left or been let go at Calvary Church. I knew that some of them felt they were deeply wronged in the way the church treated them. So I went to each of them individually and apologized on behalf of the church. My last words to Calvary Church at my last service were given in the form of a brief video. It said:

"For those I have offended in word or deed or in not doing what I said I would do, I ask your forgiveness. And for those who have offended me in word or deed or in not doing what they said they would do, please know that you are forgiven. I want to leave Calvary Church with a clear conscience."

One of the blessings of having a terminal disease is that you get the opportunity to resolve broken relationships. In pastoral ministry I have met with many families who did not have that opportunity. Had they known the person was going to die, they would have resolved their differences with that person. But now it was too late. So let me encourage you to make a list of the people whom you have likely offended over the years. Begin with your own family. Expand it to your circle of friends and those who work with you. Then ask God to give you courage to go to them and ask their forgiveness. One of the best things you can do for yourself is to resolve those relationships before you die. And one of the best things you can do for those around you is to seek their forgiveness.

Evening Promise

I am continually sinking. Is there solid ground to stand on?

> *He is the Rock, his works are perfect,*
> *and all his ways are just.*
> *A faithful God who does no wrong,*
> *upright and just is he. (Deuteronomy 32:4)*

My disease is both degenerative and terminal. The degenerative side of my disease means that it is a continual downward spiral.

It started in my right hand and arm. It has spread to my left hand and arm. It has also spread to my neck, back, stomach, and tongue. Over the last several years, the muscles in those areas have gotten weaker and weaker. About the time I begin adjusting to a specific weakness, something else gets weaker as well. There is no level ground. There are no time-outs, no reprieve.

Most terminal diseases are similar. Good news is followed by bad news, which is followed by worse news, which is followed by slightly better news, which is followed by terrible news. It's a roller-coaster ride. One day you are up, and the next day you are down. One hour you are feeling good, and the next hour you are feeling bad. You long for some stability. It's like sinking slowly in quicksand, and you long for some solid ground on which to stand.

When Moses came to the end of his earthly journey, he delivered some messages to the people of Israel. One of those messages was in the form of the song. It is found in Deuteronomy 32. The theme of that song is that God is a rock.

> He is the Rock, his works are perfect,
> and all his ways are just.
> A faithful God who does no wrong,
> upright and just is he. (Deuteronomy 32:4)

Later in the song, Moses says that God is like no other rock. "For their rock is not like our Rock, as even our enemies concede" (v. 31). What does it mean that God is *the* Rock? First, it means that he is solid ground on which you can stand. When everything around you is in constant flux, including your health, you can rely on the God who does not change. He is the Rock when everything around you is sinking sand. Second, if a rock is big enough, it offers you shade from the heat of the desert sun. God is our shade, or shelter. He protects us from the constant heat of life.

Do you feel as if you are constantly sinking? Are you longing for some stability, some solid ground on which to stand? Then look no further. God is the rock on which you can stand. Moses says,

> I will proclaim the name of the LORD.
>> Oh, praise the greatness of our God!
> He is the Rock, his works are perfect,
>> and all his ways are just. (Deuteronomy 32:3–4)

Right now say to God, "I declare that you are my God. I thank you that you are a great God. You are greater than my disease. You are my Rock. All that you do is perfect. All your ways are right. Therefore I give you praise." Then consider the words of the following hymn:

> The Lord's our Rock, in Him we hide,
> A Shelter in the time of storm;
> Secure whatever ill betide,
> A Shelter in the time of storm.

> Oh, Jesus is a Rock in a weary land,
> A weary land, a weary land,
> Oh, Jesus is a Rock in a weary land,
> A shelter in the time of storm.

> A Shade by day, Defense by night,
> A Shelter in the time of storm;
> No fears alarm, no foes affright,
> A Shelter in the time of storm.

> The raging storms may 'round us beat,
> A Shelter in the time of storm;

We'll never leave our safe retreat,
A Shelter in the time of storm.

O Rock divine, O Refuge dear,
A Shelter in the time of storm;
Be Thou our Helper ever near,
A Shelter in the time of storm.

Vernon J. Charlesworth, c. 1880

Morning Prayer

Blessed are you God our God, King of the universe.

Several years ago my oldest son and I took a course required for conversion to Judaism at a local Jewish synagogue. We took the course, not because we wanted to convert from Christianity, but simply because we wanted to understand Judaism better. Every Monday night for an entire year we listened to the rabbi instruct us on the Jewish way of living. We studied about Shabbat. We studied the various feasts. We studied what it meant to eat kosher.

One of the things we learned was the official Jewish blessing. When Christians pray over their food, they often ask God to bless it. From a Jewish point of view, this is very foolish. After all, God has already blessed the food. He sent the rain. He sent the sunshine. He provided good farmland for growing crops. And he gave farmers the ability to grow the food and bakers the ability to bake the bread. So rather than asking God to bless the food, Jews bless God for the food. At the beginning of the meal, they pray, "Blessed are you God our God, King of the universe, who brings forth bread from the earth."

The first part of the blessing is a formula that is used throughout the day in blessing God: "Blessed are you God our God, King of the universe...." They bless God for the rain, the sunshine, the wine—they even have a blessing for the cleansing of the colon. So when they go to the bathroom they pray, "Blessed are you God our God, King of the universe who cleanses the colon."

So in the midst of my disease, I began blessing God for all of the gifts of life. I use this official formula (I learned to do it in Hebrew), and I bless God for each day. I bless God for the ability to shower and clothe myself. I bless God for the ability to button buttons. I bless God for the ability to lift food to my mouth even though I can no longer do it with my right hand. I bless God for everything I can do and for every gift that comes from him.

So let me encourage you to bless God today. Use this same formula, and then add your own dimensions to it. If you prefer, you can substitute the word *praise* for the word *bless*. When you bless God, you are not adding value to God in the same sense that God blesses you. You are praising God as the source of every good and perfect gift. "Blessed are you God our God, King of the universe, who ..."

Evening Promise
Jesus is the Alpha and Omega.

"I am the Alpha and the Omega, the Beginning and the End."
(Revelation 21:6)

Jesus' statement that he is the Beginning and the End follows John's description of heaven as a place where there is no more death or mourning or crying or pain. The one seated on the throne (Jesus) says, "I am making everything new!" (Revelation 21:5) and follows that with "I am the Alpha and the Omega." Since alpha is the first letter of the Greek alphabet and omega is the last, Jesus is saying that he is the first and the last.

I know that Jesus is the Alpha in my life. He was there at the beginning. In fact, he was vitally involved in my life even before I was born.

> *I praise you because I am fearfully and wonderfully made;*
> > *your works are wonderful,*
> > *I know that full well.*
> *My frame was not hidden from you*
> > *when I was made in a secret place.*
> *When I was woven together in the depths of the earth,*
> > *your eyes saw my unformed body. (Psalm 139:14–16)*

God was deeply involved in my life from the moment of conception. He was there when I was born. He was there when I was a kid. He was there when I was a teenager. He is the Alpha in my life. But he is also the Omega. When I come to the end of my earthly journey and I am getting ready to cross over, he will be there as the Omega in my life. The God who was with me before I was born is the God who will be with me when I come to the end of my journey.

From beginning to end, God is God. From beginning to end, Jesus is Jesus. He is the First and the Last. He is the Alpha and Omega. He is the Beginning and the End. In other words, from beginning to end, Jesus is all I need. In the book of Acts (7:54–60), we read that when Stephen came to the end of his journey, Jesus was there to meet him. He said, "Look,… I see heaven open and the Son of Man standing at the right hand of God." The crowd became extremely angry and started to stone him. While they were stoning him, he prayed, "Lord Jesus, receive my spirit." Then he asked God to forgive the people who were stoning him. "When he had said this, he fell asleep."

Jesus was there at the end of Stephen's life, and the text simply says, "He fell asleep." I know that that same Jesus will be with me when I come to the end of my life, and I hope it will be said about me, "He fell asleep!"

_____

_____

_____

_____

_____

_____

_____

_____

_____

_____

_____

_____

_____

_____

_____

_____

_____

_____

_____

_____

_____

Day 10

Morning Prayer

God, I confess all known sin to you.

We know that there is a relationship between sickness and sin. "A heart at peace gives life to the body, but envy rots the bones" (Proverbs 14:30). Most people living in biblical times believed there was a direct connection between sin and sickness. If a person was sick, that meant there was unconfessed sin in that person's life. Even the disciples of Jesus believed this. "As [Jesus] went along, he saw a man blind from birth. His disciples asked him, 'Rabbi, who sinned, this man or his parents, that he was born blind?'" (John 9:1–2). Jesus dispelled this idea that sickness and sin are always connected, saying, "Neither this man nor his parents sinned,... but this happened so that the work of God might be displayed in his life" (v. 3).

Not every sickness is a result of sin, but some are. So when you are diagnosed with a terminal disease, it is a wonderful time to confess all known sin to God. When you confess your sins to God, you should not expect immediate healing from your sickness. But you can expect that a heart at peace will give life to the body, because confessing our sin leads to peace in the heart, and peace in the heart gives life to the whole body.

So make a list of all your sins. The things you said you would do that you did not do. The wrong attitudes that you have harbored toward yourself and others. The times when you directly disobeyed God. Envy. Jealousy. Malice. Lust. Pride. And a host of other things. Then confess each sin to God and ask his forgiveness. Confession is good for the soul, good for the heart, good for your life. It will free you from bondage to your past.

Evening Promise
We live in jars of clay.

We have this treasure in jars of clay to show that this
all-surpassing power is from God and not from us.
We are hard pressed on every side, but not crushed;
perplexed, but not in despair; persecuted, but not abandoned;
struck down, but not destroyed. We always carry around
in our body the death of Jesus, so that the life of Jesus may
also be revealed in our body. (2 Corinthians 4:7–10)

The city of Corinth was known for its pottery factories. They specialized in pottery that was very thin and thus fragile and easily broken. Writing to the church in this city, Paul reminds them that Christ dwells in human jars of clay. These jars of clay are fragile and easily broken, yet the treasure of Christ lives within them. My jar of clay is broken — and so is yours. I feel very much like Paul did. I am hard-pressed. I am perplexed. I am persecuted. I am struck down. The verb translated "struck down" is actually an athletic term. In wrestling it means to throw someone down on the mat. I feel as if I've been thrown down on the mat and the wind has been knocked out of me.

Paul goes on to say, "Therefore we do not lose heart. Though outwardly we are wasting away, yet inwardly we are being renewed day by day" (2 Corinthians 4:16). Paul had come to terms with an important biblical principle. As our physical health declines, our spiritual health can increase. As the physical body begins to waste away, we can be strengthened every day. This means that as my disease advances and my health declines, my spiritual life should progress. Note that this renewal is a daily thing. The renewal I experienced yesterday is not good enough for today. I need to be renewed again today. The renewal I experience today is not good enough for tomorrow. I need to be renewed in my inner being every single day. Just as my disease gets worse every day, so my spiritual life should get better every day.

So how can we be renewed every day? We are renewed through praying, reading God's Word, giving thanks to God, enjoying the friendship of others, and accepting the grace and strength of God. One of the greatest challenges faced by those with serious illnesses is that they do not feel like praying or reading or giving thanks for being around others. I have discovered in my own journey that short prayers and short Bible readings and short times with friends have a way of renewing us on a daily basis.

Paul concludes his discussion of suffering with the following: "For our light and momentary troubles are achieving for us an eternal glory that far outweighs them all. So we fix our eyes not on what is seen, but on what is unseen. For what is seen is temporary, but what is unseen is eternal" (2 Corinthians 4:17–18). Note that Paul calls his troubles "light and momentary." When you read this entire chapter, you discover that his troubles were certainly not light. But Paul understood that in comparison to eternity, they were light and momentary. So is my disease. So I'm focusing on the eternal—not the temporary.

Day 11

Morning Prayer

God, help me to get lost in the wonder of who you are.

When I first received the diagnosis of my disease, I wanted to be anointed with oil and prayed over by those who actually believe in healing. So I called my good friend Wayne Benson, former pastor of the First Assembly of God in Grand Rapids. I knew he believed in healing, so I asked him and his wife to come over and anoint me with oil.

The evening they came was one of the most powerful evenings in my entire life. Wayne and his wife spent several hours with my wife and me. They talked about healing. They told stories of people in their church who had been anointed with oil and had been miraculously healed. They also told stories of people who were anointed with oil who had not been miraculously healed. Before Wayne anointed me with oil, he gave me this advice: "Do not become obsessed with healing. Get lost in the wonder of God, and who knows what God will do for you." *Get lost in the wonder of God.* I had been lost in the wonder of my disease. Now I was being told to get lost in the wonder of God.

So I have tried to lift my focus above my disease and keep it connected to the wonder of God. The God who created and sustains the universe. The God who created me. The God from whom I derive life. The God who knows more about my disease then all the physicians in the world combined. The God who has the power to touch my body and reverse the ravages of this disease.

Recently I was camping overnight far from any signs of civilization. We set up our tents near a small lake in the wilderness. The sky was clear, and I had never seen stars quite as brilliant as on that night. It was as if I could reach out and touch them. I lay on the ground for a long time looking at the stars. Then I realized that the God who created all the stars was the God who loves me and proved his love by sending Jesus. This God cares about me. He did not send his Son to save the stars. He sent his Son to save me. It was one of those moments when I felt lost in the wonder of God. Still I pray, "God, help me to get lost in your wonder."

Evening Promise
He is all you need.

I know what it is to be in need, and I know what it is to have plenty. I have learned the secret of being content in any and every situation, whether well fed or hungry, whether living in plenty or in want. I can do everything through him who gives me strength. . . . And my God will meet all your needs according to his glorious riches in Christ Jesus. (Philippians 4:12–13, 19)

These are some of the most amazing promises in all the Bible: we can do everything through Jesus Christ who infuses us with strength, and God will meet all of our needs all of the time. These promises are especially vital when you are facing a serious illness. What I need more than anything else is the knowledge that I can do all things and that God will meet all of my needs. Paul wrote these promises under very difficult circumstances—he was in prison. Think about the actual words contained in each promises.

"I can do everything." Sometimes I can hardly get out of bed in the morning. Sometimes I can hardly face my family and friends. Sometimes I can hardly deal with the issues at work. Sometimes I cannot face the uncertainties of tomorrow. There are many things I can hardly do. But God promises that through Jesus Christ, I can do everything! The key is to understand that what I do I do not do in my own power. Rather, I do it in the strength that God gives. So the key to doing everything is relying on God's power and not my own strength.

"My God." The one who infuses me with strength is not some abstract spirit being floating around in space. He is "my God." He knows me. He created me. He knows what's happening in my body. He knows every detail of my disease. He knows my future. This is my God!

"Will meet all your needs." This is an absolute promise from the absolute God. It is not speculation. It is not that "maybe" he will meet my needs. The truth is that he will meet all my needs. What I am facing may be different than what you are facing. Your needs may be different than my needs. Your situation may be different than my situation. But this promise transcends our differences. It will meet your needs, my needs, and the needs of everyone who relies on God.

"According to his glorious riches." God is never bankrupt. Out of his glorious riches he provides for my needs, your needs, everyone's needs. And when he has provided all of our needs, his riches are no less depleted than when he started.

"In Christ Jesus." "Praise be to the God and Father of our Lord Jesus Christ, who has blessed us in the heavenly realms with every spiritual blessing in Christ" (Ephesians 1:3). All that

God does for us in meeting our needs he does because we are in Christ Jesus.

Do you need strength? God has promised to strengthen us. Do you have needs? God has promised to meet all of your needs out of his glorious riches in Christ Jesus. Say these verses over and over. Memorize them. Keep on saying them. I cannot think of any verses more appropriate for those of us who struggle with serious illness.

Day 12

Morning Prayer
God, give me something to laugh about.

I remember reading a story of a physician who was very sick and in the hospital. He was in terrible pain, and no medicine seemed to ease his suffering. The doctors ran every possible test yet were completely baffled. They could not figure out the source of the disease, and they could not ease the level of pain. For this physician the future seemed hopeless. As he lay there in his hospital bed, he began watching television. He watched the Three Stooges. And as he watched them, he started to laugh. He immediately realized that when he laughed, his pain went away. So he began watching a lot of Three Stooges films. The more he laughed the better he felt. He literally laughed his way back to health.

When you are terminally ill, there is very little to laugh about. Everything about your disease and about your future is dark and depressing. Every decision you make impacts your life and your future. But don't forget to laugh. The day after I was diagnosed with ALS, I was at the local athletic club running. I usually ran at the same time, and so I got to know the other runners who ran at that time. As I turned a corner, I passed a young woman I knew as a regular runner and asked how she was doing. "I'm just dying," she replied. "Me too!" I said. The rest of the way around the track I laughed and laughed and laughed. And it felt good.

A few days later I arrived at my office, and sitting in front of the door was a beautiful flower arrangement. I thought, *That is really something. Someone has thought of me and my disease and just wants to encourage me.* I bent over and looked at the card and found out that it was sent to me by a funeral home. I laughed and laughed and laughed.

But I have to tell you that the moments of laughter are few and far between. So I pray on a regular basis, "God, give me something to laugh about." When I want to watch television, I usually opt for a comedy. When I want to watch a movie, I usually opt for a comedy. Last night we ate dinner with some very close friends. We spent most of the evening laughing together. I cannot tell you how wonderful that feels when you're facing a terminal illness. So laugh a little today.

Evening Promise
Learn to rejoice — whatever the circumstances.

> *The stone the builders rejected*
> *has become the capstone;*
> *the LORD has done this,*
> *and it is marvelous in our eyes.*
> *This is the day the LORD has made;*
> *let us rejoice and be glad in it.*
> *(Psalm 118:22 – 24)*

On the night Jesus was betrayed, he gathered with his disciples in an upper room to celebrate the Passover. During the meal he broke bread and told his disciples that the bread represented his body, which would be broken for them. Then he took the wine and declared that this was the wine of the new covenant in his blood for the forgiveness of sins. At the end of the meal, they sang a song and went out into the night. What did they sing? They sang from the Hallel, including Psalms 113–18. The first two psalms are sung at the beginning of the meal, and the rest are sung at the end of the meal.

In the first part of Psalm 118, the psalmist speaks of the enduring love of God. "Give thanks to the LORD, for he is good; his love endures forever" (v. 1). In fact, the phrase "his love endures forever" is repeated four times. The psalm also speaks of the rejection and suffering of Jesus. "The stone the builders rejected has become the capstone" (v. 22). Then the psalm says, "This is the day the LORD has made; let us rejoice and be glad in it" (v. 24).

At the Last Supper, Jesus was facing the cross. He alone knew the terrible road that lay ahead. In addition to all the physical pain of crucifixion, he knew that he would bear the sins of the entire world. In a moment of time, he would suffer eternal hell on behalf of us. He knew that in the darkness of that hour, God the Father would turn his back on him and he would be forced to say, "My God, my God why have you forsaken me?" (Matthew 27:46). The perfect Son of God would take my sin upon him. Then he would suffer the penalty of that sin and endure all of the justice and wrath of God against all sin for all time. He alone knew what was ahead. And yet he could say, "This is the day the LORD has made; let us rejoice and be glad in it."

If Jesus could sing hours before he faced the cross, I can sing facing what I face. He said that he would be betrayed by one of his own. Peter would deny him three times. All of the disciples would flee. He would also be falsely accused and condemned to die. He would carry his own cross and be nailed to it. He would shed his blood for the forgiveness of sins. And at the moment of deepest despair, God the Father would turn his back on him. Still he could sing, "This is the day the LORD has made; let us rejoice and be glad in it."

"God, you know I am not facing the cross. I have not been betrayed or rejected. I am not bearing the sins of the world. And in my deepest despair, you have not abandoned me. So help me to sing!"

This is the day,
This is the day
That the Lord hath made,
That the Lord hath made.
We will rejoice,
We will rejoice
And be glad in it,
And be glad in it.
This is the day that the Lord hath made.
We will rejoice and be glad in it.
This is the day,
This is the day
That the Lord hath made.

Les Garrett

Day 13

Morning Prayer
God, help me to ignore the negative statements of others and remind me that they mean well.

When you are terminally ill, people say a lot of dumb and negative things to you. I know they mean well, but they have no clue about the impact those statements make on you. Some people say to me, "Oh, you have a terminal illness. Well, you know, we're all dying." What they fail to understand is that while we have an intellectual knowledge that we are dying, those of us who are terminally ill *feel* that we are dying. And there is a huge difference between knowing it and feeling it. The twitches and weakness in my muscles and the things that I can no longer do are constant and continual reminders that my clock is ticking and my days are numbered. I feel in the depths of my being that I am dying. I find little comfort from those who are not dealing with a terminal illness who gladly say, "Well, we're all dying."

Other people will try to encourage me with the following: "My uncle died of the same disease in six months. Maybe you would like to talk to my aunt for some encouragement." I don't want to talk to someone who died quickly of this disease. If I'm going to talk to anyone with this disease, I'm going to talk to someone who has fought it and delayed it and is still alive! Others have said, "You need to watch the movie about Tuesdays with Morrie. It will really encourage you." Again, I don't want to watch a movie about someone who is dying of this disease. If I'm going to be encouraged, I want to be encouraged by someone for whom the disease is slow-growing and who has survived for an extended period of time.

At first I was semi-offended by people who gave me negative advice. But then I realized that they don't know what I'm going through. They really do want to help. And they think that their advice will be of great help to me. They want to do something, and this is the best they can come up with. So I really should not be offended. I have learned to thank them even though I do not follow through on their advice. One of the dangers is accepting negative advice and letting it impact the way you think about the disease. So I pray, "God, help me to ignore the negative statements of others and remind me that they mean well."

Evening Promise
Learn to deal with a thorn in the flesh.

To keep me from becoming conceited because of these surpassingly great revelations, there was given me a thorn in my flesh, a messenger of Satan, to torment me. Three times I pleaded with the Lord to take it away from me. But he said to me, "My grace is sufficient for you, for my power is made perfect in weakness." (2 Corinthians 12:7–9)

We do not know what the apostle Paul's thorn in the flesh was. We do know that it had something to do with his flesh. Perhaps it was a disease or a disability. We do know that it bothered him and humbled him. He says that it kept him from becoming conceited. Disease will do that. It will knock all the pride out of you.

Paul did what we all do when we are faced with a thorn in the flesh—he prayed. Three times he "pleaded with the Lord to take it away from [him]." We know that Paul had a gift for healing. When Paul was on his way to Rome to stand trial before Caesar, he was shipwrecked off the island of Malta. The father of the chief official of the island became sick, so Paul went to see him. Paul laid his hands on him and prayed for him and healed him. "When this had happened, the rest of the sick on the island came and were cured" (Acts 28:9). Paul had the power to heal, and that healing was exercised in the context of prayer. Even though Paul had the power to heal others, he did not heal himself. He prayed, but he was not healed.

Instead, God gave a remarkable answer. "My grace is sufficient for you, for my power is made perfect in weakness." God did not answer Paul's prayer. At least he did not answer it in the way Paul had anticipated or asked. But he did answer it. God responded to Paul by reminding him that his grace and power would be sufficient. In fact, Paul would discover the power of God through his own personal weakness. Paul went on to say, "Therefore I will boast all the more gladly about my weaknesses, so that Christ's power may rest on me. That is why, for Christ's sake, I delight in weaknesses, in insults, in hardships, in persecutions, in difficulties. For when I am weak, then I am strong" (2 Corinthians 12:9–10).

In weaknesses.

In insults.

In hardships.

In persecutions.

In difficulties.

I'm not sure I feel the same way Paul did. I have never been excited about weaknesses, insults, hardships, persecutions, and difficulties. But Paul was excited. Why? Because he understood that at the time of his greatest weakness, he would discover the greatest amount of God's power. And God's power always compensates for our weakness. When it comes to my own thorn in the flesh, I keep asking God for relief and healing. I have asked more than three times. I know that if God chooses not to heal me, he will give me the greatest strength and power to deal with this weakness. In this I can be confident.

Day 14

Morning Prayer
God, help me not to be afraid, for you are with me.

I am not afraid of being dead. After all, I know where I'm going. But I am afraid of getting dead. Nearly everyone I have talked to who has a terminal disease feels the same way. We know where we are going, but we are afraid of the process we have to go through to get there. Whenever I think of that process, I began to sink into despair. And the more I think about it, the deeper I sink. Soon after my diagnosis I came across some verses that have sustained me in my darkest hour.

"God has said, 'Never will I leave you; never will I forsake you.' So we say with confidence, 'The Lord is my helper; I will not be afraid'" (Hebrews 13:5–6).

"God has said, 'Never will I leave you; never will I forsake you.' So we say with confidence, 'The Lord is my helper; I will not be afraid'" (Hebrews 13:5–6).

"God has said, 'Never will I leave you; never will I forsake you.' So we say with confidence, 'The Lord is my helper; I will not be afraid'" (Hebrews 13:5–6).

"God has said, 'Never will I leave you; never will I forsake you.' So we say with confidence, 'The Lord is my helper; I will not be afraid'" (Hebrews 13:5–6).

"God has said, 'Never will I leave you; never will I forsake you.' So we say with confidence, 'The Lord is my helper; I will not be afraid'" (Hebrews 13:5–6).

If you read this verse one time and skipped all the other readings, go back and reread them. Whenever I would sink into despair, I would take a five-minute time-out. I would repeat this promise over and over for the entire five minutes. By the end of the five minutes, I would begin to believe what I was saying. You can make these verses your prayer for the day. You can make these verses your prayer whenever you fear the future and the whole process of dying. In fact, as I mention in Day 3, I wrote these verses on a three-by-five card and put them on my mirror so that every morning they would be the first thing I would see when I went into the bathroom. When my youngest son went to Iraq with the Army National Guard, I took the card off the mirror and gave it to him. I wanted him to know that God would be with him every mile he traveled.

In my own experience, simply saying the verse one time had little impact. It was only as I repeated it over and over and over again that I actually began to believe that it was true. So I pray, "God help me not to be afraid, for you are with me."

Evening Promise

My Redeemer lives, and I will see him with my own eyes.

> "I know that my Redeemer lives,
> and that in the end he will stand upon the earth.
> And after my skin has been destroyed,
> yet in my flesh I will see God;
> I myself will see him
> with my own eyes—I, and not another.
> How my heart yearns within me!" (Job 19:25–27)

The story of Job is one of the most puzzling stories in all the Bible. In a matter of days, Job lost his children, his health, and his wealth. He lost everything. In despair his wife told him to "curse God and die" (Job 2:9). We know from the story that Satan is the one who caused all of these tragedies in Job's life. We also know that God allowed Satan to do it. If God is all-powerful and if God loves us, why would he allow Satan to destroy Job's life? The entire book of Job is devoted to these questions, and there is no completely satisfactory answer.

Job responded to all of this injustice, saying:

> "I know that my Redeemer lives,
> and that in the end he will stand upon the earth.
> And after my skin has been destroyed,
> yet in my flesh I will see God;
> I myself will see him
> with my own eyes—I, and not another.
> How my heart yearns within me!" (Job 19:25–27)

Job understood that God was his Redeemer. He had a personal relationship with God. Because of that personal relationship with God, he could trust God even when life did not make sense. Job also realized that there was more to life than the temporal. He declared that when his skin was destroyed, yet in his flesh he would see God. He went on to emphasize this point: "I myself will see him with my own eyes."

Job's reality was shaped by these two ideas: first, he had a relationship with God, and second, one day he would see God. While neither of these ideas fully explain the terrible suffering he went through, they did sustain him in the midst of the struggle. In the midst of my own struggle, I need to keep the same ideas in mind. I would like to know the answer to the questions, why me, why now, and why this disease; but I am fully aware that I may never fully grasp satisfactory answers to these questions. They will go with me to the grave. What I do know, however, is that God is with me, and when this life is over, I will be with God.

So whatever you are facing, remember that God is with you now. Remember that if you have committed your life to Christ, in this moment, facing this disease, God is with you — your Redeemer lives. And when this life is over, you will go to be with God.

Day 15

Morning Prayer

God, remind me that it is "if," not "when."

*"Whatever is true, whatever is noble, whatever is right,
whatever is pure, whatever is lovely, whatever
is admirable—if anything is excellent or praiseworthy—
think about such things." (Philippians 4:8)*

For many years one of our Christmas traditions was to get together with several other couples for dinner. It was one of the highlights of our year. We always went to the same house and had the same couples seated around the dinner table. We ate. We talked. We laughed. We cried. It was a wonderful evening. The last time we did it, the hostess at whose house we met was terminally ill with cancer. She was one of the most remarkable women I have ever met. She was a wife, a mom, a grandmother, and a college professor. At that time she had been struggling with cancer for several years.

She refused to call her struggle a battle with cancer. She argued that when you are in a battle, you deploy all of your resources toward the battle. She did not want to do that. She believed that there was much more to her life than just cancer. If she were to put all of her energies into fighting cancer, her life would automatically shrink, so she continued to live life to the fullest. She was funny. She was stubborn. She was one of the most courageous people I have ever met.

Sitting at dinner that night, the woman next to me asked about the prospects for my disease. I began telling her about the weakness in my right hand. "Eventually I will lose the ability to use my fingers. So last week my doctor told me I should begin writing with my left hand so that when my right hand quits working, I will still be able to write." The hostess who had cancer was sitting across the table listening to the conversation. As soon as I reported what my doctor had said, she said, "It's 'if,' not 'when.'"

What a profound insight! I was thinking that it was only a matter of when. But the truth is, at that point, I could still write and do everything with my right hand. I had not lost the ability to use it. But I had descended into negative thinking, assuming that the time would come when I would lose the use of my hand. My friend reminded me that the real issue was "if" not "when." This insight offered a profound difference in thinking. To think "when" is negative. To think "if" is positive. At that moment I discovered why my friend had outlived all the doctors' prognoses: she was living with "if" not "when." I often tend to be a negative thinker. I think about the worst-case scenario and then realize that anything less than that is a blessing. So now I pray, "God, remind me that it is 'if,' not 'when.'"

Evening Promise
There is a time for everything.

There is a time for everything,
and a season for every activity under heaven:
a time to be born and a time to die,
a time to plant and a time to uproot,
a time to kill and a time to heal,
a time to tear down and a time to build,
a time to weep and a time to laugh. (Ecclesiastes 3:1–4)

There is a time for everything. Are you going through a very difficult time? Hang on. It's about to get better. Are you going through a really good time? Hang on. It's about to get worse. Life is never the same from day to day. I especially like the idea from Ecclesiastes that there is "a time to weep and a time to laugh." I have spent a great part of my life laughing. After all, I'm Irish, and the Irish love to laugh.

Have you heard the story about the Irishman who came to the United States and lived in Boston? Every Tuesday he went down to the pub and ordered four pints of Guinness and drank all of them. This routine went on for months. Finally, the bartender asked, "Is there a special significance to the fact that every Tuesday you come in for four pints of Guinness?" "Yes, there is," the Irishman said. "Every Tuesday I used to go down to the pub with my three friends in Ireland, and we drank a pint each. Then I immigrated to the United States. So every Tuesday I come down to the pub and drink a pint for each of them." After about a year, the Irishman came in one Tuesday and ordered three pints instead of four. He did this for several weeks. Finally, the bartender asked him, "Has something happened to one of your friends? For the last couple of weeks you've only been drinking three pints and not four." "Not at all," the Irishman said. "My friends are all okay. I only drink three pints because I've given up drinking for Lent." (Please don't be offended at a story about pubs and drinking. I am Irish you know. Have a good laugh and keep reading.)

I love life and I love to laugh. But there is more to life than laughing. There is also a time to cry. And I have done my share of crying these last five years. I have cried over my personal loss of mobility. I have cried because I can no longer do the things I used to be able to do. I have cried because this disease has forced me to resign from pastoring a church. I have cried because if I talk too much, I begin slurring my words. I have cried because I can barely type on a computer. I have cried as I have watched my wife and kids deal with this disease. I have cried for what it has done to them as much as I have cried for what it has done to me. I have learned that there is both a time to laugh and a time to cry.

Sickness, disease, and health are all part of the cycle of life. They are something that every single one of us will face. Life is not all good all the time. Nor is life all bad all the time. Life is a mixture of good and bad, sickness and health, laughter and crying. So what have I learned? When life is good, give thanks to God. When life is bad, ask God to help you. When you are sick, pray for healing. When you are healthy, thank God for it. When it's time to laugh, laugh from the depths of your belly. And when it's time to cry, don't hold back. These are the realities of the world in which we live. I would prefer good times, health, and laughter. But if they were not balanced out with bad times, sickness, and crying, then the good times would not seem so good, the health would not seem so wonderful, and the laughter would not seem quite so funny. So today I plan to laugh a little and cry a little.

Day 16

Morning Prayer
God, help me to leave a legacy for my family.

My last service at Calvary Church was very emotional. The auditorium was packed and people were standing around the edges. Several overflow rooms were filled. After nineteen years, it had come to this. The choir sang. People shared how God had changed their lives. Kids from the inner city performed a rap song in my honor. Other pastors shared. People gave video greetings. Then my wife and I knelt at the front, and we were commissioned for service to the church at large. I was surrounded by thousands of people whom I loved and who loved me. Many of them had come to faith under my ministry. Others had grown in the Lord. Some had gone into full-time ministry as a result of my preaching. It was a rewarding, enriching, and powerful evening.

At the end of the service, I walked up the steps of the platform with my family, out the back door, down the hallway, and into the parking lot, then drove home. Physically and emotionally I could not stand and shake hands with all the people who were there that night, so I decided just to leave. When I got to the car, I had this incredible feeling of relief. I left behind Calvary Church and its thousands of people. I walked out with just my family. It was a powerful reminder that in the journey ahead what really mattered was my family. So I pray, "God, help me to leave a legacy for my family."

During my years at Calvary Church, I conducted more than four hundred funerals. I always met with the family ahead of time to talk about what they would like said and done. During my meeting with the family, I asked them about the deceased person. I took notes on what they said and tried to include that information in my meditation at the funeral. Sometimes the response was immediate and overwhelming. The spouse, children, and grandchildren talked about what the person meant to them and how he or she influenced their lives. There was usually lots of laughing and lots of crying as they reflected on the person's life. Sometimes, however, there was a very awkward silence. Very few things were said about the person. I could tell immediately that the deceased person had a very negative influence on the family and that the family did not want to get honest with what the deceased was really like. The person had failed to leave a legacy for his or her family.

Since I have only a limited time left, I want to make sure that I pour my time and efforts into my own family. I do not want the thousands of people at Calvary Church to speak well of me as much as I want my family to speak well of me. After all, when the pressure is on and you are facing an uncertain future, you walk away from the thousands of people and you walk out with your own family. So I pray, "God, help me to leave a legacy for my family."

Evening Promise

We all need a friend to go with us.

"Go in peace, for we have sworn friendship with each other in the name of the LORD, saying, 'The LORD is witness between you and me, and between your descendants and my descendants forever.'"
(1 Samuel 20:42)

Jonathan and David were the best of friends. Jonathan was the son of King Saul and legal heir to the throne, but God had rejected Saul's family line because of Saul's disobedience. Instead, David had been anointed by Samuel as the new king of Israel. Saul hated David and for many years attempted to have David killed. Still Jonathan and David were the best of friends.

On one occasion Saul invited David to a banquet at the palace. David feared for his life and decided not to go. David asked Jonathan to look out for his best interest. If Saul expressed that he missed David at the banquet, then it would be safe for him to go. But if Saul became angry, then David's life was in jeopardy. Saul did become angry, so Jonathan met with David in secret to tell him what had happened at the banquet. They both knew that Saul intended to kill David. Then "Jonathan said to David, 'Go in peace, for we have sworn friendship with each other in the name of the LORD, saying, "The LORD is witness between you and me, and between your descendants and my descendants forever."'"

David learned that when someone is out to kill you, you need a good friend. When you have a disease that is out to kill you, you also need a good friend. My closest friend is my spouse. She has been a tower of strength. She has given me encouragement, strength, and hope. I also have several other friends who are walking with me. One of them is a woman who has the same disease I have. Although she is now in a wheelchair, her stubborn attitude and her unwillingness to give in to the disease have greatly encouraged me. We try to meet once a month, and I am always encouraged in talking with her.

David's son Solomon talked about the importance of a good friend. "Two are better than one, because ... if one falls down, his friend can help him up" (Ecclesiastes 4:9–10). In addition to human friends, we also have a friend who is "closer than a brother" (Proverbs 18:24). This friend is Jesus. "Greater love has no man than this, that he lay down his life for his friends. You are my friends if you do what I command. I no longer call you servants, because a servant does not know his master's business. Instead, I have called you friends, for everything that I learned from my Father I have made known to you" (John 15:13–15). Even if you do not have a human friend to walk with you through your struggle, you have a divine friend who will never leave you or forsake you. And this divine friend knows everything you are thinking and feeling. He knows the depth of your struggle. He understands your fear about the future. He knows everything about you. And he is still your friend. So be encouraged. God has said, "Never will I leave you; never will I forsake you" (Hebrews 13:5).

Morning Prayer
God, remind me that this life is not all there is.

Even though I have sometimes failed miserably, for most of my adult life my passion has been to love and serve God. For nineteen years I served as the senior pastor of Calvary Church. My passion was to teach the Bible and love people. I tried faithfully to do just that. I have had a number of close friends in ministry who chose to do otherwise. Either they morally defaulted or they bailed out on God, the Bible, and the church. They don't care about loving or serving God. They are not interested in teaching the Bible or loving people. They have chosen their own paths. I am terminally ill, and they are healthy and happy. Sometimes this really bothers me. After all the years of trying to love and serve God, is this what I get? And what about those who have walked away from God? What do they get? Apparently they get a life free of disease. This seems profoundly unfair to me. But then I remember that there is more to life than here and now. There is eternity. And the just Judge of all the universe will hold everyone accountable for what he or she has done and said.

I have met a number of times with the leading teacher of Kabbala in our community. Kabbala is a collection of mystical teachings of rabbinical origins, often based on an esoteric interpretation of the Hebrew scriptures. Kabbala teaches that there are ten separate worlds and that the world in which we live is only one of those worlds (called *malchut*). This means that the present physical reality in which we live is less than 10 percent of the ultimate reality. While I am not an advocate of Kabbala, and I don't fully understand it, I think it has an important point to make: the world in which we live is not the ultimate reality. This is why Paul says, "I consider that our present sufferings are not worth comparing with the glory that will be revealed in us" (Romans 8:18).

So I leave my questions of unfairness with God. I leave the apparent injustices with him. I must not be too attached to the present physical reality, for it is not the ultimate reality. The ultimate reality is heaven, eternity, God himself. As the old gospel song says, "This world is not my home; I'm just passing through." So I pray, God, remind me that this life is not all there is.

Evening Promise
Heaven is better by far.

"Now the dwelling of God is with men, and he will live with them. They will be his people, and God himself will be with them and be their God. He will wipe every tear from their eyes. There will be no more death or mourning or crying or pain, for the old order of things has passed away." (Revelation 21:3–4)

In Revelation 21 the apostle John records the words of the voice he heard coming from the throne in heaven, giving a description of life in the new Jerusalem. One of the great promises John heard is that there will be no more death or mourning or crying or pain. No more ALS. No more cancer. No more chemotherapy. No more hospitals. No more funeral homes. At that time death will be conquered. Disease will be conquered. Crying will be conquered. Pain will be conquered. What a day that will be!

Whenever I think about heaven a number of questions come to mind. First, will we know each other in heaven? The answer is yes. We will be known in heaven as we are known down here. When Moses and Elijah appeared with Jesus on the Mount of Transfiguration, the disciples knew who they were. We will not only know each other in heaven, we will know other people as well.

Another question is, where is heaven? Some scholars have argued that heaven is at the farthest end of the cosmos. But recently some others have suggested that heaven may be right around us in a sphere that we cannot see, taste, or touch. When Stephen was martyred, he said, "Look, ... I see heaven open and the Son of Man standing at the right hand of God" (Acts 7:56). Did Stephen see to the farthest reaches of the cosmos? Maybe. But perhaps heaven was right around them, and for a brief moment he was able to see in this new dimension. Whether heaven is at the end of the cosmos or right around us, we can be sure of this one thing: it is a real place.

Perhaps the most compelling question is, what is heaven like? My father has a favorite description of heaven from the words of Paul. "I am torn between the two: I desire to depart and be with Christ, which is better by far; but it is more necessary for you that I remain in the body" (Philippians 1:23–24). My father's favorite description of heaven is found in those three words "better by far." What is heaven like? It is better by far. It is better than the best moments we have here with our family and friends.

I think of some of the wonderful times I've shared with my family. I think of the time we were all in Ireland together and decided to play golf (more like pitch and putt). We played by the ocean on the northern coast of Ireland. It was pouring rain and the wind was blowing off the ocean. We ran from hole to hole and shot the shot. Just thinking about that time makes me laugh. And there were many other wonderful times that we shared together. What is heaven like? It is better by far than the best of what earth has to offer. My father was so impressed with these words of Paul that when my mother died, he had them inscribed on her gravestone. The inscription reads: "Eileen McKnight Dobson—better by far."

Paul was able to say, "I consider that our present sufferings are not worth comparing with the glory that will be revealed in us" (Romans 8:18). So as I face the struggles and challenges of this day, I know they in no way compare to the glory that will be revealed in me. And I know that when I get to heaven, it will be "better by far"!

Day 18

Morning Prayer
God, help me to accept help when needed.

Pastoral ministry is a life of giving, and this is true of some other professions as well. Pastors are on call twenty-four hours a day, seven days a week. Thus I do much better at giving than I do at receiving. Receiving is a challenge. Even as I struggle with this disease, it is difficult to ask for help. Increasingly, I have difficulty buttoning the buttons on my shirts. It takes me about fifteen minutes to button my shirts by myself. Sometimes I get stuck on one of the buttons. It would be much easier to ask my wife to help me, but I continually resist the urge. I don't like to ask for help.

I am reminded of the story in John 13 of Jesus and his disciples in the upper room the night before the crucifixion. Jesus begins washing the disciples' feet. When he gets to Peter, Peter objects. "Lord, are you going to wash my feet?" Jesus responds, "You do not realize now what I am doing, but later you will understand." Peter then says, "No,... you shall never wash my feet." Peter refuses Jesus the opportunity to model true servanthood. His refusal is ultimately an act of pride, for he is disallowing Jesus the opportunity to do something for him. Likewise, when I refuse help, I am disallowing someone else the opportunity to serve and in so doing am demonstrating pride.

I want to do as much as I can for as long as I can, but there are times when I need help. By refusing help, I am denying someone else the opportunity to serve me. And like Peter, I end up looking foolish. So when I am struggling to button my buttons, I need to ask my wife to help me. When I cannot do something, I need to have courage to admit it. So I pray, "God, help me to accept help when needed. Remind me that when I refuse help, I'm acting independently and ultimately I'm arrogant. Remind me that I am refusing others the opportunity to exercise the gift of serving."

Evening Promise

Jesus is preparing a place for us.

"Do not let your hearts be troubled. Trust in God;
trust also in me. In my Father's house are many rooms;
if it were not so, I would have told you. I am going there to
prepare a place for you. And if I go and prepare a place for you,
I will come back and take you to be with me that you also
may be where I am." (John 14:1 – 3)

The word *troubled*, as used by Jesus on the night of the Last Supper, means to be agitated. I think I know how they felt. Several years ago our cat climbed into the dryer on top of some warm clothes. My wife came along, not knowing the cat was in the dryer, closed the dryer door, and pushed the button to further dry the clothes. She heard this terrible thumping in the dryer and knew something was wrong. So she stopped the dryer and opened the door. The cat staggered out with hair going in every direction and a totally dazed look on his face. I felt the same way when I was diagnosed. I felt as if I had been lying quietly on top of some warm clothes in the dryer. Then someone came along, closed the door, and pushed the button. When the door finally opened, I staggered out with a totally dazed look on my face. I was troubled. But Jesus tells his disciples not to be troubled. Then he gives them some more reasons why.

He says, "In my Father's house are many rooms" (John 14:2). I prefer the King James Version translation—"In my Father's house are many mansions"—because I like the idea of mansions better than I do rooms. But the actual word in Greek means rooms, not mansions. The idea is connected to the ancient marriage ceremony. When two people wanted to get married, their parents got together and worked out a marriage covenant. Once the covenant was signed, it was as if they were married. After signing the covenant, the groom would go back to his father's house and build a room for his future wife. Usually this room was built on the second or third floor of the family dwelling. When he had finished building the room, he would then go and collect his wife, and there would be a great wedding feast. Finally, he would bring her back home to live in the room he had built.

Jesus told his disciples that he was going away to prepare rooms for them. Like the ancient groom, when the rooms were finished, he would come and get them. Then they would live with him for all eternity. So even though Jesus has gone back to the Father, he has not forgotten about us. In fact, he is busy preparing a room for us. And at the proper time, he will come back and get us.

Audio Adrenaline, a contemporary Christian group, had a popular upbeat song in the 1990s entitled "Big House" that has brought comfort to millions. Here are some of the words.

Come and go with me to my Father's house.
Come and go with me to my Father's house.

It's a big, big house,
with lots and lots of room.
A big, big table,
with lots and lots of food.
A big, big yard,
where we can play football.
A big, big house,
it's my Father's house.

We are not alone. Our future is bright. Jesus has promised to come and get us.

Day 19

Morning Prayer
God, I would still rather be shallow and healthy.

When I first started out in ministry I chose the following verse as my life's verse: "Therefore we do not lose heart. Though outwardly we are wasting away, yet inwardly we are being renewed day by day" (2 Corinthians 4:16). I liked the last part of the verse: "yet inwardly we are being renewed day by day." I interpreted this to mean that it is important to focus on your spiritual journey every single day. You need to read the Bible and pray every day. You need to love God and serve others every day.

I still like this verse, but now it speaks to me at a whole different level. Now I focus on the first part of the verse, "Though outwardly we are wasting away." This is where I am in life. My body is slowly wasting away. As the neurons die and the signal no longer gets from my brain to my muscle, my muscles begin to atrophy. I can no longer do all of the things I used to do. But the promise of this verse is that even though this may be happening in my body, I can still grow spiritually and be "renewed day by day."

I will gladly testify that this has happened in my life. When you are facing a terminal disease, you either get better or you get bitter. My walk with God has been greatly deepened by the experience I have faced. I can testify with Paul. "Praise be to the God and Father of our Lord Jesus Christ, the Father of compassion and the God of all comfort, who comforts us in all our troubles, so that we can comfort those in any trouble with the comfort we ourselves have received from God" (2 Corinthians 1:3–4). My life has been radically changed by the suffering that I have endured. I'm a different person than I wanted to be before the disease. I believe I am more like Christ as a result of this struggle. But I have to be honest: I would still rather be shallow in my spiritual walk and healthy than spiritually mature and sick. So I pray, "God, you know I would rather be shallow and healthy, but I trust you to grant me the grace to continue the journey."

Evening Promise

Don't forget God's benefits.

Praise the LORD, O my soul;
all my inmost being, praise his holy name.
Praise the LORD, O my soul,
and forget not all his benefits—
who forgives all your sins
and heals all your diseases,
who redeems your life from the pit
and crowns you with love and compassion,
who satisfies your desires with good things
so that your youth is renewed like the eagle's.
(Psalm 103:1–5)

When you have a serious illness, it is easy to forget all of God's benefits. The disease is all you can think about and all you can talk about. It begins to consume your entire life. Eventually it takes over your life. And when it takes over your life, you begin to lose perspective. You begin to forget all the benefits that God has given you. So let me remind you.

I have two ears to hear. I have two eyes to see. I have a tongue to speak. I have two hands to work. I have two legs to walk. I have two feet on which to stand. Even though a good number of my muscles do not work the way they used to, they still work a little. Even though when I'm tired I begin to slur my words, I can still be understood. Even though my fingers can no longer type well or button my shirt well, I can still type a little and somehow manage to button my shirts. *So I thank you, God, for all of these benefits.*

I have plenty of water to drink. I have plenty of food in the refrigerator. I have plenty of clothes to wear. I have a bed to sleep in at night. I have a warm house in the middle of winter. I have indoor plumbing. I have electricity. I have several televisions. I have several radios. I have a car. And I can still drive. I can still lift food to my mouth — although I can no longer do it with my right hand. My left hand still works. I can still swallow. I can still breathe. I can still hold my wife in my arms. *So I thank you, God, for all of these benefits.*

I have a supportive wife. I have three beautiful children. The oldest is married, and they have two children who are my grandchildren. I have another who is recently married. I have yet another who is in the Army National Guard and has served one tour in Iraq. They all know the Lord. They all love the Lord. And they all want to serve the Lord. *So I thank you, God, for all of these benefits.*

In Psalm 103, David lists several benefits that he has received from God. They apply to you as well. He forgives all your sins. He heals all your diseases. He has redeemed your life from the pit. He crowns you with love and compassion. He satisfies your desires with good things. Your youth is renewed like the eagle's. *These blessings belong to me too, so I thank you, God, for all of these benefits.*

God's grace has brought me to this point in my life. He has not failed me yet. And his grace will sustain me today. And whatever tomorrow holds, I know that his grace will be sufficient for that. He is the God of yesterday, today, and tomorrow. He has done great things in my life. He is doing great things in my life. And he will do great things in my life. *So I thank you, God, for all of these benefits.*

God, you love me with an everlasting love. You have forgiven all of my sins and iniquities, and you will not remember them against me again. You have given me the righteousness of Jesus Christ. You have given me the Holy Spirit to live within me. You have given me your Word to guide me in my earthly pilgrimage. You are working all things together for my good. You have placed me in a community of faith so that when I suffer, all the community suffers with me. And when I rejoice the whole community rejoices with me. So thank you, God, for all of these benefits.

Friend, have you ever taken time to consider the benefit package? Have you ever thanked God, like David did, for all of the benefits that he has given you? Thanking God for all of his benefits helps you put your disease into perspective. I do not want my whole life to be consumed by this disease, nor do I want to lose my perspective of what God has done for me, is doing for me, and will do for me.

Morning Prayer

God, remind me that there is more to life than this disease.

When you are diagnosed with a terminal disease, it consumes your thinking—from the time you wake up in the morning until you drift off to sleep at night.

We live in the information age. Everything a person would ever want to know about ALS is available on the Internet with the click of a mouse. For the first few months after my diagnosis, I read thousands of pages of information about ALS. I even borrowed the official medical textbook for ALS from my doctor. I read it several times from cover to cover. I became a walking encyclopedia of medical knowledge about ALS. I am sure that I knew as much about the disease and maybe even more than most neurologists. It consumed me.

One evening my wife and I went out for a cup of coffee at our favorite coffee shop. I ordered a cappuccino that came in a rather large cup. As we were sitting there sipping our coffee, I said to my wife, "Look at this: I can still lift this heavy cup to my mouth without help." As soon as I said this, my wife broke down crying. She said, "Is that all you can talk about? Every time we talk, you talk about the disease. Isn't there more to life than your disease?" She was right. That's all I thought about. That's all I read about. And that's all I talked about.

We spent the rest of the time talking about what we could do to change. I agreed that I would limit the amount of time I spent on the Internet researching the disease. We agreed that we would not talk about the disease unless we mutually agreed to discuss it. We would talk about other matters—the house, my job, our kids, the grandkids, her job, the Bible, prayer, and a host of other topics.

I was discovering that I could not judge my life exclusively by this disease nor view my life exclusively through the lens of this disease. Yes, I was terminally ill, but I was still a husband, dad, grandfather, and pastor. And in the process of dealing with the disease, I had unintentionally abandoned these roles. It was now time to recapture them. That night at the coffee shop was a major turning point in my journey with this disease. Now I pray, "God, remind me that there is more to life than this disease."

Evening Promise
Don't forget your source.

Hezekiah trusted in the LORD, the God of Israel.
There was no one like him among all the kings of Judah,
either before him or after him. He held fast to the LORD
and did not cease to follow him; he kept the commands
the LORD had given Moses. (2 Kings 18:5–6)

Hezekiah became a king of Judah when he was twenty-five years old, and he reigned for twenty-nine years in Jerusalem. There was no one like Hezekiah before him or after him. Early in his reign he removed the high places and smashed the sacred stones. "He broke into pieces the bronze snake Moses had made, for up to that time the Israelites had been burning incense to it" (2 Kings 18:4).

The bronze snake represented an important symbol in Jewish history. When the children of Israel were wandering in the desert, they began complaining against God and Moses. God sent venomous snakes among them, and many of them died. The people asked Moses to pray for them so that God would take away the snakes. God instructed Moses to make a bronze snake and put it on a pole. Anyone who had been bitten by a snake and looked to the snake would live (Numbers 21). Looking to the snake was an act of faith, and God honored that act of faith by healing the person who looked.

Even Jesus referred to this incident. In a conversation with a religious leader named Nicodemus, he said, "Just as Moses lifted up the snake in the desert, so the Son of Man must be lifted up, that everyone who believes in him may have eternal life" (John 3:14–15). What healed the people in the desert? Their faith. They looked to the snake by faith. What saves people today? Their faith. We look to Jesus by faith.

By the time of Hezekiah, the people had forgotten about faith and had turned the snake into a symbol of worship. In fact, they were offering incense to the bronze snake. They had lost their connection with the source. It was God who healed them—not the snake. God simply used the snake as a symbol. The people were worshiping the symbol not the source, so Hezekiah destroyed the symbol.

I find that I make the same mistake in my own life. In facing my own disease, I often have more faith in symbols then I do the source—God himself! I pay attention to doctors and medicine. I'm constantly trying to learn the latest developments in ALS and the newest results of research. I pay attention to diet and exercise because I know how vital they are in promoting good health. I pay attention to my immune system. I want to do everything I can to improve it so I can fight this disease. While these are certainly important tasks, the danger is that in pursuing them I forget that my ultimate hope is God. I can turn these tasks into bronze snakes. I can spend all of my time and effort in pursuing them and little or no time in pursuing God. So I ask God to help me keep everything in balance.

Day 21

Morning Prayer

God, help me to hear your voice in the midst of my struggle.

Hear, O Israel: The LORD our God, the LORD is one. Love the LORD your God with all your heart and with all your soul and with all your strength" (Deuteronomy 6:4–5). In Judaism this is the opening statement of the Shema. It is repeated every morning and every evening by religious Jews. In biblical times it was the first thing parents taught their children to say. It was also to be the last words Jews repeated before they died. So the Shema was something that began and ended life, and began and ended every day. "Hear, O Israel: The LORD our God, the LORD is one." This is also the central statement of Jewish theology, which speaks of the uniqueness and oneness of God.

This phrase is called the Shema because the opening verb in the Hebrew is *Shema*. It means "to listen." Jews began and ended every day by listening to God. Yet this verb means even more—it has the idea of diligently studying so that one might obey God. I have found it very difficult in the midst of a terminal disease to listen to God. I listen attentively to the doctors. I pay attention to all of the nuances of my own body. I know when I'm feeling better and when I'm feeling worse. I know when I have lost strength in a particular muscle group. I read and study all of the latest research on ALS. I talk with others who have the same disease. I tend to pay attention to everybody but God.

Therefore I have started saying the Shema every morning and every evening. It reminds me of the importance of listening to God. Throughout the day I will hear many different voices, but I must begin each day by deliberately trying to pay attention to God. After the Shema, I read some verses from the Bible and commit the day to God. Then throughout the day I try to pay attention to what God is telling me through the people I meet. I find that it is a daily struggle. On the one hand, I'm facing the constant reality of my disease. But on the other hand, I am also trying to pay attention to God. So I pray, "God, help me to pay attention to your voice in the midst of my struggle."

Evening Promise
Who will go with me?

And God said, "I will be with you." (Exodus 3:12)

The story of the life of Moses is remarkable. He was hidden by his parents when Pharaoh ordered that all of the male babies of the Hebrews be murdered. He was placed in a basket and set among the reeds on the Nile River where he was discovered by Pharaoh's daughter. She took him as her own son and reared him in the palace. One day Moses saw an Egyptian and a Hebrew fighting. He intervened and killed the Egyptian. When Pharaoh heard about this, he wanted Moses killed, so Moses fled into the desert of Midian. There he met Jethro, the priest of Midian, and married one of his daughters whose name was Zipporah. After the birth of their son, Moses said, "I have become an alien in a foreign land" (Exodus 2:22).

I know that feeling. I feel as if I'm an alien. I have a terminal disease, and I'm out of step with all of my healthy friends. I feel like I don't quite belong anymore. I feel like I'm in a foreign land with a completely different culture and language. It's a place I never intended to live. I feel as if I've left the warmth and security of Pharaoh's palace and found myself on the back side of the desert.

But it is precisely on the back side of the desert where God met with Moses. In Exodus 3 we read that one day while he was tending the sheep, he saw a bush that was burning. What attracted him to this bush was that while it burned it was not consumed. God called his name from the bush, "Moses! Moses!" God then told him that he had heard the cries of his people in Egyptian slavery, and he informed Moses that he was going to send him back to Egypt to set his people free. Moses immediately objected. "Who am I, that I should go to Pharaoh and bring the Israelites out of Egypt?" But God persisted. "I will be with you." Then Moses asked, "Suppose I go to the Israelites and say to them, 'The God of your fathers has sent me to you,' and they ask me, 'What is his name?' Then what shall I tell them?" God replied, "I AM WHO I AM" (Exodus 3:10–14). This is the name of the God who will also go with you: "I AM WHO I AM."

This name is from the Hebrew verb "to be." It speaks of the eternal existence of God, reminding us that God simply is. He's timeless and eternal. Whenever we feel like aliens in a foreign land, or whenever we find ourselves on the back side of the desert, it is important to know that the God who speaks to us is the God who is timeless and eternal. He is not limited by time and space or by sickness or disease. Whether in the palace of Pharaoh or on the back side of the desert, he is still God.

Some of the Jewish translations of the Hebrew Bible translate this phrase "I shall be as I shall be." This gives us hope not only for the present but also for the future. What God was yesterday he is today. What God is today he will be tomorrow. He is the same yesterday, today, and forever. So be encouraged. God was, God is, and God shall be. Wherever you have been, wherever you are, and wherever you are going, remember that God is with you. And the God who is with you calls you by name. He called Moses by name from the burning bush, and he calls you by name as well.

Morning Prayer

God, teach me to be thankful even in these circumstances.

Be joyful always; pray continually; give thanks in all circumstances, for this is God's will for you in Christ Jesus" (1 Thessalonians 5:16–17). Notice how Scripture encourages you and me to "give thanks in all circumstances." It does not say, "Give thanks *for* all circumstances." Although I have heard some Christians give thanks for a terminal disease such as cancer or MS, I have never been able to do that. Maybe it's a lack of spiritual maturity, but I have never managed to be thankful for ALS. I believe this text is calling us to be thankful *in* our circumstances, not *for* them. And there is a huge difference.

I'm learning each day to be thankful *in* my circumstances. And I have much for which to be thankful. Since I am normally rather pessimistic, it is all the more important for me to learn to give thanks. I usually focus on how bad things are, not on how good they are. I'm trying to focus more on the good and to be thankful for it. Recently I began thanking God specifically for every item he had given me. I went through my closets and thanked him for every tie, every shirt, and every suit. I'm not talking about a general thanksgiving, but about thanking God one item at a time. I did the same for my shoes, socks, T-shirts, and underwear. Then I thanked him for each piece of furniture in the room. I thanked him for the bottom sheet on the bed and the top sheet. I thanked him for the pillow and pillow cases. I thanked him for the blanket. I thanked him for the mattress and box springs. I thanked him for the bed. I went around the room thanking God for everything individually.

This took quite a while. By the time I got through, I was overwhelmed with how good God had been to me. And this was only one room in the house. I did not include all of the books I had (it would take a long time to thank God individually for each book). And these were only material gifts. I did not include my family and friends. I did not include all of the spiritual blessings that are mine through Christ Jesus: the Word, the Spirit, salvation, sanctification, and all of the blessings that come to us as a result of our relationship with Christ. Today I want to be thankful, so I pray, "Teach me, God, to be thankful even in these circumstances."

When you sit down to make a list of all of your blessings and thank God for them, you will be overwhelmed at his goodness and greatness and kindness.

Evening Promise
All things work together for good.

And we know that in all things God works for the good of those who love him, who have been called according to his purpose. For those God foreknew he also predestined to be conformed to the likeness of his Son, that he might be the first born among many brothers. And those he predestined, he also called; those he called, he also justified; those he justified, he also glorified. (Romans 8:28–30)

If one more person tells me that all things work together for good, I'm going to scream! Many well-meaning people have told me not to worry; after all, God will work all things together for good. But from where I'm sitting, things don't look so good. It's easy to quote this verse when everything is going well. The challenge is to quote it and believe it when everything goes bad. When the doctor tells you that there is nothing he can do for you, is God still working things out for your good? When the doctor tells you to put your house in order because you're in the process of dying, is God still working things out for your good? I know that God loves me. And I know that I love God in return. This text tells me that this same God who loves me is working all things together for good. I find this a difficult truth to swallow.

If God loves me and God is for me and God is working all things for my good, how can I be sure of it in the face of this disease? Paul answers this question: "If God is for us, who can be against us?" (Romans 8:31). The issue is, how do we really know that God is for us? After all, in the face of this disease, it is difficult to see how God could be for me. But Paul answers this question as well: "He who did not spare his own Son, but gave him up for us all—how will he not also, along with him, graciously give us all things?" (v. 32). The ultimate proof that God is for us is found at the cross. When I am tempted to question whether God is with me, I go back to the cross. God demonstrated once and for all that he loved us and that he is for us by giving his Son to be our Savior. And Paul says that if God was for us at the cross, he is also for us in our daily lives.

Paul goes on to say that nothing can ever separate us from God's love. "I am convinced that neither death nor life, neither angels nor demons, neither the present nor the future, nor any powers, neither height nor depth, nor anything else in all creation, will be able to separate us from the love of God that is in Christ Jesus our Lord" (Romans 8:38–39). Even though I may not understand how God works everything for good, I am confident that I am never beyond the reaches of his love. In the middle of his statement on love, Paul adds the little phrase "nor anything else in all creation." This means that there is absolutely nothing that can separate us from God's love in Christ Jesus—not sickness, not disease, not death. Nothing!

So even though I may not understand how God is working things for my good, I know that he is. He has proved his love for me at the cross. And the cross guarantees that he will give to me whatever grace I need for today. And besides all that, nothing will ever separate me from his love. So while I cannot explain how God works, I can rest in his love and in his grace. When someone says to me, "Don't worry, Ed; God is working all things together for good," I have to remind myself that they are speaking the truth—a hard truth, a mysterious truth, an inexplicable truth, but nonetheless, the truth.

Day 23

Morning Prayer
God, give me your shalom.

> *"The LORD bless you*
> *and keep you;*
> *the LORD make his face shine upon you*
> *and be gracious to you;*
> *the LORD turn his face towards you*
> *and give you peace."* (Numbers 6:24–26)

A terminal disease will rob you of your peace. I find myself distraught about the future. I find myself fearful of the process of dying. I find myself troubled about the thought of leaving my family behind. I get discouraged whenever I think that I am in the prime of my life in terms of work but am on disability. While others work, I find myself imprisoned with my own disabilities. And in the middle of all of this, it's hard to have shalom.

Some people think that shalom is the absence of conflict and war. Others think that shalom is being free of trouble and difficulty. But this is not the biblical concept of shalom. Shalom is wholeness with God, others, and yourself. It is becoming what God intended for you in the present moment. You can have shalom and be in conflict. You can have shalom in the midst of trouble. You can have shalom when you're facing a terminal disease. How? By simply asking God to give it to you. And the mystery that I cannot explain is that God indeed grants shalom in the midst of suffering. Shalom comes when God turns his face toward us. And I am grateful to know that God's face is toward me even in the midst of my suffering.

Recently I came across a shalom blessing: "Shalom to you. Shalom to your house. Shalom to all that is yours." I like that. I need the shalom of God in my own life. I need the shalom of God in my house. And I need the shalom of God to invade everything that is mine. And so I pray for shalom for me, my house, and all that is mine.

Evening Promise
The Lord is my shepherd.

The LORD is my shepherd, I shall not be in want.
He makes me lie down in green pastures,
he leads me beside quiet waters,
he restores my soul. (Psalm 23:1–3)

Abraham, Isaac, Jacob, and Joseph were all shepherds. So was King David. So was the prophet Amos. Jesus called himself a shepherd. He said, "I am the good shepherd. The good shepherd lays down his life for the sheep" (John 10:11). Later in the New Testament, the Greek word translated "pastor" is actually the word for shepherd. Many people in my congregation called me Pastor Ed or Pastor Dobson. However, they could have called me Shepherd Ed or Shepherd Dobson.

When Jacob and his brothers went down to Egypt to be with Joseph and to live in the land, Joseph gave them instructions about how to address Pharaoh and how to answer his questions. "When Pharaoh calls you in and asks, 'What is your occupation?'

you should answer, 'Your servants have tended livestock from our boyhood on, just as our fathers did.' Then you will be allowed to settle in the region of Goshen, for all shepherds are detestable to the Egyptians" (Genesis 46:33–34).

Why did God not reveal himself as a pharaoh? After all, the pharaoh was the most powerful person in the ancient world, and if God wanted to reveal himself as the most powerful god, it would have been logical for him to reveal himself as a pharaoh. But instead, God revealed himself as a shepherd—the one occupation that was detestable to the Egyptians.

The Egyptians lived along the Nile River where water was plentiful and crops could be grown. They preferred the city life. Shepherds, on the other hand, lived in the desert where water was scarce and crops could not be grown. It was a difficult life. Shepherds were nomads. They wandered from place to place looking for water and food for their flocks. From an Egyptian point of view, this was a terrible life. But from God's point of view, it best described God's relationship with his people. He is the shepherd and we are the sheep.

Recently I was in Israel and spent some time watching a shepherd in the desert taking care of some sheep. He was by himself and was leading a flock of about a hundred sheep and goats through the desert to places where they could eat. I stood and watched him for quite a while. He was extremely patient as he moved the flock along the wadi. When I started to get close to the flock, he pulled out a flute and began to play music. Later I asked him why he had played music for the sheep. He told me that as I approached the sheep, they became very agitated and upset. He had learned that when the sheep were agitated, if he played music for them on his flute, they would quiet down.

God is like that shepherd. He leads me, guides me, and provides for me, and he knows where I need to go. When I get agitated, he does whatever is necessary to calm me. Even if it means pulling out a flute and playing music. David writes:

> Even though I walk
>> through the valley of the shadow of death,
> I will fear no evil,
>> for you are with me;
> your rod and your staff,
>> they comfort me. . . .
>
> Surely goodness and love will follow me
>> all the days of my life,
> and I will dwell in the house of LORD forever. (Psalm 23:4, 6)

Morning Prayer

God, give me the grace I need to die.

We do not do well when it comes to death. In fact, after a person dies, we do everything we can to make it look as if they are not really dead. We embalm them. We dress them up. We put makeup on their faces. We have special lighting at the funeral home. And we say, "Doesn't she look good?" *Look good?* She's dead. But we have done everything we can to make it look as if she is still alive.

We are a culture obsessed with life and with looking young. We pay very little attention to death and dying. But we all are going to grow old and die. My advantage is that I know I am dying and my time is limited. Those who do not have a terminal disease are actually at a disadvantage. They are dying, but they don't really know it. So for me the issue is, how am I going to die? Am I going to die with dignity and grace, or am I going to contradict everything I have believed and said in my final act on planet Earth? For me this is not a theoretical question. It's real!

One of the stories that encourages me is the story that Jesus told about the rich man and Lazarus. Both of them died. "The time came when the beggar died and the angels carried him to Abraham's side" (Luke 16:22). When it came time for the beggar to cross from this life into the next, God dispatched angels to carry him into eternity. Apparently angels are part of the transportation ministry of heaven. Whenever a believer is about to die, God dispatches angels to lovingly and gently carry that person from this life into the life to come. This encourages me. It means that when I come to the end of my earthly journey, I will not face it alone. God will be there. And God will dispatch angels to carry me from this life into the life to come. Until that moment, I pray, "God give me the grace I need to die."

Evening Promise

When you come to the end of your journey,
God will be there to take care of you.

"The time came when the beggar died and the angels
carried him to Abraham's side." (Luke 16:22)

Over the years I have spent time with many people as they came to the end of their earthly journeys. On a number of occasions, I was with the person when he or she actually died. As I look back on those experiences, I realize what a privilege it was to be there. I felt as if I was standing on holy ground. The barrier between the temporal and the eternal seemed particularly thin. It was as if I could reach out and touch the face of God. I cannot explain those experiences logically. I can simply tell you that I was aware of God's presence in a much more powerful way than at any other time in my life.

I promised my mother when she was dying that she would not die alone. I promised that I would be with her. And so for the last several days of her life, I spent all of my time with her. A few days before she passed away, she said to me, "Ed, get my coat. Wilma is out in the hall waiting for me, and I need to go."

Wilma was a very close friend of my mother who was diagnosed with cancer about the same time. She and my mom had shared their journeys together for several years, but she had passed away a number of months before my mother. And now with my mother coming close to the end herself, she thought that Wilma was out in the hall waiting for her to come out. Maybe it was the increasing doses of morphine, but I happen to believe that my mother was already beginning to see across to the other side.

So what happens when a person comes to the end of the earthly journey? Jesus told the story of the rich man and the beggar. When it came time for the beggar to die, the angels of God carried him to Abraham's side. I find great encouragement in the thought that whenever a believer is about to leave this life and enter the life to come, God sends angels to carry him or her to heaven. When I come to the end of my earthly journey and I'm about to leave this life and enter the life to come, God's angels will be there to meet me and to carry me into his presence.

So even though I am a little anxious about how things will happen at the end, I have the assurance that God will be there to meet me. I was with my mother when she breathed her last breath. It was a sacred moment. Even though I could not see them, the angels were there to carry my mother's soul from her diseased wracked body into the presence of the eternal God. And when it's time for me to go, the angels will be there for me as well. Maybe God will send the same angels for me as he sent for my mother. I hope so!

Day 25

Morning Prayer
God, give me courage to choose to live and not to die.

I remember the day as if it were yesterday. It was close to Christmas. I was sitting on the porch of our house watching the snow come down. I was thinking that this might be my last winter and my last Christmas. The more I thought about it, the more depressed I became. Then I came to the following text from the words of Moses:

"This day I call heaven and earth as witnesses against you that I have set before you life and death, blessings and curses. Now choose life, so that you and your children may live, and that you may love the LORD your God, listen to his voice, and hold fast to him. For the LORD is your life, and he will give you many years in the land he swore to give to your fathers, Abraham, Isaac and Jacob" (Deuteronomy 30:19–20).

The words "choose life" jumped off the page. Moses was telling the Hebrews that if they obeyed the Torah, they would live. But if they did not obey the Torah and were "drawn away to bow down to other gods and worship them," they would "certainly be destroyed" (vv. 17–18). So the Hebrews could choose to live. Or they could choose to die.

It seemed to me that I was in a similar situation. Faced with a terminal disease, I could choose to live, or I could choose to die. The choice was up to me. *Choose life. Choose life. Choose life. Choose life. Choose life.* I needed to hear those words over and over and over again. I could give up and give in to the disease, and by doing so, choose to die, or I could choose to live. So sitting on the porch that winter afternoon, I prayed, "God, give me the courage to choose to live and not to die."

On one of my recent visits to the University of Michigan clinic, I told one of the doctors, "If this disease gets me, it will get one of the healthiest people it has ever gotten." The doctor laughed. "Most of the people who sit in the chair where you sit go home, give up, and die. Your attitude is the kind of attitude that will extend your life." Choosing life is making daily choices that promote living and not dying.

I recently took three semesters of biblical Hebrew at a local seminary. Even though I may not be around much longer, I wanted to continue growing in my understanding of the text. I wanted to keep living. Living is planting a garden, wallpapering a new room, taking a computer course—doing anything that will promote living and not dying. It is putting together a photo album, sewing a blanket, knitting a sweater, spending time with your family. *Choose life. Choose life. Choose life. Choose life.* I still pray, "God, give me courage to choose to live and not to die."

Evening Promise

Sometimes you have to take the next step by yourself.

> *"Do not be afraid. Stand firm and you will see*
> *the deliverance the LORD will bring you today.*
> *The Egyptians you see today you will never see again.*
> *The LORD will fight for you; you need only*
> *to be still." (Exodus 14:13–14)*

There was good news and there was bad news. The good news was that the children of Israel had been delivered from Egyptian bondage. They had left Egypt and were free from slavery. God had intervened in miraculous ways, and now Moses was leading them out of the land. The bad news was that the Egyptian army was pursuing them, the mountains were on either side of them, and the Red Sea was before them. They were trapped. And so they complained, "Was it because there were no graves in Egypt that you brought us into the desert to die? What have you done to us by bringing us out of Egypt?... It would have been better for us to serve the Egyptians and to die in the desert!" (Exodus 14:11–12).

Moses responded to the people in the same way we would have responded to them. "Do not be afraid. Stand firm and you will see the deliverance the LORD will bring you today. The Egyptians you see today you will never see again. The LORD will fight for you; you need only to be still" (vv. 13–14). This is exactly how I feel—trapped. The Egyptians are behind me, the Red Sea is before me, the mountains are on either side, and there is nowhere to turn. So what do I do? I want to stand still and see God miraculously intervene on my behalf. I want God to do what only God can do. I want him to deliver me.

But this is not what God had the children of Israel do. He said to Moses, "Why are you crying out to me? Tell the Israelites to move on. Raise your staff and stretch out your hand over the sea to divide the water so that the Israelites can go through the sea on dry ground" (vv. 15–16). In other words, God was saying, "Stop standing still. Take the next step. Move forward in the face of impossibility. And when you do, I will be there to divide the Red Sea." While I would prefer to stand still and see the deliverance of God, there are times when I have to take the next step, however difficult that step may be, and move forward. It is only when I take the next step that God moves in a miraculous way and divides the Red Sea.

I have a good friend who was engaged to be married. Shortly before her wedding, her fiancé was killed in a terrible accident at work. It was a devastating blow. With one phone call her whole life changed. Her dreams and hopes for the future were shattered. She said, "I get up in the morning. I take a shower, get dressed, and put on my makeup. Then I tell God, I've done everything I can do. Now the rest of the day is up to you." She understood what the children of Israel understood. We have to do what we can do and then leave the rest to God.

In my own journey, I have discovered the same truth. I have to get up every morning and get dressed, but the rest of the day is up to God. If I do not take the first step, I will never see the deliverance of God. Some people do not get up in the morning, do not get dressed, and do not put on their makeup. They lay there waiting for God to intervene. But they never see his deliverance. So get out of bed, get dressed, put on your makeup, and leave the rest to God.

Day 26

Morning Prayer
God, give me wisdom to know what to do.

The Internet is a wonderful blessing and a terrible curse. When I was first diagnosed, I spent a lot of time on the Internet researching ALS. After a while, the volume of information began to overwhelm me. The more I learned about the disease, the more I sank into despair. I was learning way too much information about my disease, and the overload of information was playing tricks with my mind. I would read about symptoms that I currently did not have, but once I read about them, I began thinking that I was already experiencing them. I envied those people who chose not to read anything about the disease and just took whatever happened as it happened. They were unaware of what would happen in their future. Unfortunately, I was at the other extreme and knew too much.

The Bible says, "If any of you lacks wisdom, he should ask God, who gives generously to all without finding fault, and it will be given to him" (James 1:5). So I began praying for wisdom. How do I respond to all of this information and the gloomy prognosis for my disease? God answered my prayers by reminding me that I should limit the time I spend researching the disease. So I limited my time to thirty minutes a day. I found this to be most helpful.

Another area where I desperately needed wisdom was in response to the many people who talked to me or wrote to me.

In our church there is every kind of independent marketer of health and wellness products. They all felt they had the answer to my particular situation. Not wanting to offend any of them, I needed wisdom to know what to do. So I asked God. Eventually, he gave me wisdom. I began asking people for written material about the products they were selling. I told them I would read the material and decide whether their products were appropriate for me to take. Dozens of people offered me their products. Actually, I did not take any of their products, because I found no evidence that they had helped someone with my disease.

One of the problems of having a terminal disease is that you do not have a lot of time to make decisions. The longer you wait, the more time bomb is ticking in your body and ready to explode. You feel this incredible pressure to do something and to do it quickly. Time is not on your side. You are faced with a choice between traditional medicine and alternative medicine. You are faced with choices in traditional medicine and choices in alternative medicine. And you do not have a lot of time to decide what to do, so you need to pray continually, "God, give me wisdom to know what to do." And God has promised that he will give you wisdom.

Evening Promise

God is the God of the past and the God of the present.

Therefore, since we have been justified through faith,
we have peace with God through our Lord Jesus Christ,
through whom we have gained access by faith into this
grace in which we now stand. (Romans 5:1–2)

In the fifth chapter of Romans, the apostle Paul talks about God's past blessings and God's present blessings. In verse 1 he says, "Therefore, since we have been justified through faith...." In verse 11 he says, "Not only is this so, but we also rejoice in God through our Lord Jesus Christ, through whom we have now received reconciliation." God has done some things for us in the past, and God is still doing things for us in the present.

The past blessings. Paul says that we have been "justified." This means that we have been declared righteous by God himself. This righteousness comes through the death, burial, and resurrection of Jesus Christ. We are sinners, and Jesus took our sin upon himself. He is absolutely perfect, and he exchanged our sin for his righteousness. This is what it means to be justified. And that justification is by grace and through faith.

The present blessings. In this chapter Paul gives a list of our present blessings. First, he says that we have peace with God through our Lord Jesus Christ. The idea of peace is more than the absence of conflict or war. It means wholeness. It means that we become everything that God created us to be. We are at peace with God, with ourselves, with others, and with creation.

Second, we have "gained access by faith into this grace in which we now stand" (v. 2). Grace is the unmerited favor and loving-kindness of God. We were saved by grace, the favor and kindness of God. But we also are continuing in grace. The favor and kindness of God are what keep us going each day. We were saved by grace. We now stand in grace.

Third, we have hope. "And hope does not disappoint us, because God has poured out his love into our hearts by the Holy Spirit, whom he has given us" (v. 5). The present reality of hope comes at the end of a section that deals with trouble and suffering. Paul says, "We also rejoice in our sufferings," and goes on to say that "suffering produces perseverance; perseverance, character; and character, hope" (vv. 3–4). It is precisely in the midst of suffering that we begin to realize the hope that God gives us each day. And hope will never disappoint.

I am grateful for my salvation. I was eleven years old when I invited Jesus Christ into my life to be my Savior and Lord. At that moment I was declared righteous through faith in Jesus Christ. My salvation is secure. I know where I'm going when I die. My struggle, however, is with today. Paul reminds us in this chapter that there are three things that we can be confident of today. First, we can be confident that we have peace with God. We can experience the wholeness of God. Second, we can be confident that we have access into God's grace. Another way of thinking of grace is the idea of strength: we have access into God's strength today. Third, we have hope. And that hope is all the more significant because it comes in the face of suffering and difficulty. So I can make it today. The God who declared me righteous in the past, is the same God who is walking with me today. And that God gives me peace, grace, and hope. He is the God of yesterday and the God of today.

Day 27

Morning Prayer
God, I don't feel like praying.

Why is it that when you are facing a critical illness, you do not feel like praying? You would think that prayer would be your first response. You would think that you would pour yourself into prayer with greater passion than ever before. But I discovered that it was very hard to pray. I did not feel like praying. I did not know what to say. I could not force myself to pray.

I did, however, discover two compelling truths that help put prayer in perspective. First, the Holy Spirit is praying for me. "In the same way, the Spirit helps us in our weakness. We do not know what we ought to pray for, but the Spirit himself intercedes for us with groans that words cannot express" (Romans 8:26). Just because I do not feel like praying does not mean that no prayer is being offered in my behalf—the Holy Spirit is interceding for me. So I can rest assured that I am not forgotten by God. The Spirit reflects my struggle by interceding with groans.

The second truth is that others are praying for me. James, in the book that bears his name, reminds us that when we are critically ill we are to call for the elders of the church to pray over us and anoint us with oil. He adds this promise: "The prayer of a righteous man is powerful and effective" (James 5:16). Even when I cannot pray, others are praying for me. This is what the body of Christ is all about. When one suffers we all suffer with that person. We carry each other's burdens. And one of the ways we do that is by praying for those who cannot pray for themselves.

One of the most encouraging things I've experienced is children writing to tell me they are praying for me every day. The faith of children is powerful, for it is uncluttered by the struggles of adulthood. They truly believe that God hears and answers prayer and that he is capable of healing any disease. So when I cannot pray myself, I can rest in the fact that others, including children, are praying for me.

When someone says to me, "I'm praying for you," I find this to be very encouraging, providing they are indeed praying for me. One of the greatest gifts you can give someone who is terminally ill is a gift of prayer. So I pray, "God, I don't feel like praying. But I rest in the truth that others are praying for me, and the Holy Spirit is interceding for me with groans that words cannot express." That is enough to get me through one more day.

Evening Promise

Praying the Lord's Prayer helps when you find it hard to pray.

> "Our Father in heaven,
> hallowed be your name,
> your kingdom come,
> your will be done,
> on earth as it is in heaven.
> Give us today our daily bread.
> Forgive us our debts,
> as we also have forgiven our debtors.
> And lead us not into temptation,
> but deliver us from the evil one." *(Matthew 6:9–13)*

My earliest religious experiences were among the Plymouth Brethren. They were wonderful people. They were also very antiliturgical. They were against formal written prayers and against the saying of the Lord's Prayer or repeating of the Apostles' Creed. They avoided anything that seemed liturgical. Of course they had their own "liturgies." They said and did things a certain way, and the same people always seemed to be involved. As a result of my early experiences with them, I have always felt uncomfortable with formal written prayers, the saying of the Lord's Prayer, and the reciting of the Apostles' Creed. Among the Plymouth Brethren, we considered these kinds of things as the repeating of vain and empty words.

I changed my mind about "liturgical things" when I was diagnosed with ALS. I quickly found out that when you are seriously ill, praying becomes difficult. Until I was diagnosed, I had a very organized system of praying. It included reading the Bible, praying for certain people daily, and praying for certain people and situations on a specific day of each week. I would write out the requests in my prayer book, and then I would circle them when God answered. But after I was diagnosed, I did not have the strength or energy to do what I had always done with prayer. So first thing in the morning, I would simply pray the Lord's Prayer. Throughout the day as I struggled, I would repeat the Lord's Prayer. When I got in bed at night and was ready to go to sleep, I would pray the Lord's Prayer one more time. And I discovered something amazing: the repeating of the Lord's Prayer brought a peace into my life that cannot fully be explained.

Our Father in heaven. I'm a dad. I would do anything for my children, including laying down my life for them. If I care that much for my children, how much more does God my Father care for me? And as my heavenly Father, he has all the resources of deity at his disposal. There is nothing he cannot do.

Hallowed be your name. To hallow God's name means to set it apart. It means that your driving desire is for God to be uplifted and honored. Even in the midst of my disease, God's glory is far more important than my specific struggle. In fact, God will be glorified as I live through the struggle.

Your kingdom come, your will be done on earth as it is in heaven. The kingdom of God is the rule of God in our lives. When we ask for the kingdom to come and the will of God to be done, we are essentially asking that God rule in our lives and in our communities and that his will would be accomplished.

Give us today our daily bread. Notice that this request is a first person plural. As I pray for my own needs today, I am praying for the needs of others as well.

Forgive us our debts, as we also have forgiven our debtors. We all need to forgive those who have offended us. One of the advantages of having a terminal disease is that you are forced to examine your own life and your relationships with others. One of the great blessings is seeking the forgiveness of God and going to people you have offended and seeking their forgiveness as well.

And lead us not into temptation, but deliver us from the evil one. We need to ask God for his leadership in our lives. As God leads, we are to ask him to deliver us from the evil one, Satan.

If you do not feel like praying, let me suggest that you pray the Lord's Prayer. You may take time to reflect on each of the requests and pray it in your own words. Or you may simply repeat the words to God. You will discover the remarkable power and peace that come through the saying of this ancient prayer.

Morning Prayer

God, give me the confidence that you are in control.

We know that in all things God works for the good of those who love him, who have been called according to his purpose.
(Romans 8:28)

Plenty of people have quoted Romans 8:28 to comfort me. Usually the people who quote me this verse have a very good life. They are not facing a terminal illness. Their lives have not fallen apart. Their family is intact. So they are confident of the goodness of God and the way he works in our lives. As a result, they want to impose this verse on me. Sometimes they simply say, "Remember Romans 8:28." They use the verse as a magic pill that will make everything fall in place. It is as if when you quote this verse, everything will be okay.

The fundamental problem is that from where I sit, things are not working out very well. My life is coming to an end. I will miss my children and grandchildren growing up. I will miss my spouse. I will miss the significant events in the lives of my family and friends. Not to mention that the dying process itself is dismal. I have yet to meet someone who did not fear that process—myself included. So when someone comes up to me and says, "All things work together for good," these sound like empty words designed to make that person feel good and make me feel worse.

But God is either in control or he is not in control. Either he is at work in the events of my life or he is not. For whatever reason, he has dealt me this hand to work with. I do not like the hand, nor would I want to give it to anyone else, but it is what God has given me to work with. So I pray, "God, help me to trust that you are ultimately in control of my life and this disease." This is not an easy prayer to pray. It contradicts the daily reality of my own experience. For if I were God, I would never put anyone through what I am going through. Yet in a way that I cannot explain, God is in control of the details of my life, so I ask him to help me trust him one day at a time.

Evening Promise

God is my rock and my deliverer.

> *"The waves of death swirled about me;*
> *the torrents of destruction overwhelmed me.*
> *The cords of the grave coiled around me;*
> *the snares of death confronted me.*
> *In my distress I called to the LORD;*
> *I called out to my God.*
> *From his temple he heard my voice;*
> *my cry came to his ears." (2 Samuel 22:5–7)*

David composed the preceding words near the end of his life. They express my innermost thoughts and feelings. I feel like I'm standing in the ocean with the waves of death surrounding me. I feel like I'm caught in a trap—the snares of death confront me. It is a completely helpless feeling. What David did is what we should do—he called out to God for help. And what kind of God was there to help him?

The LORD is my rock, my fortress and my deliverer;
   my God is my rock, in whom I take refuge,
He is my shield and the horn of my salvation, my
    stronghold. (Psalm 18:2)

God is my rock, my fortress, my deliverer, my shield, my horn of strength, my salvation, my stronghold, my refuge, and my Savior. David goes on in this song of praise to describe God's power. "The earth trembled and quaked" (v. 7). "He parted the heavens and came down" (v. 8). "He shot his arrows and scattered the enemies, great bolts of lightning and routed them" (v. 14). This God is an all-powerful God. There is nothing that he cannot do.

He reached down from on high and took hold of me;
   he drew me up out of deep waters.
He rescued me from my powerful enemy,
   from my foes, who were too strong for me.
(Psalm 18:16 – 17)

Having a terminal disease is like drowning in deep water. And just as you are about to go under, God reaches down from on high and takes hold of you. I visualize reaching up with my right hand, which is very weak, and taking the hand of God, which is not weak but is all-powerful. As long as my hand is in his hand, I'm okay. Well I'm not exactly okay. I still have this disease. And I still feel like I'm drowning. I still feel like the waves of death are all around me. But as long as I hold the hand of the creator of the universe, everything will be okay.

David concludes with a joyful explosion of praise:

"The LORD lives! Praise be to my Rock!
   Exalted be God, the Rock, my Savior!" (2 Samuel 22:47)

As long as God lives, I have hope for today, hope for tomorrow, and hope for eternity. As long as God is my rock, I will not sink into the depths. As long as God is my Savior, I know that ultimately deliverance will come. It may be in this life or it may be in the life to come, but either way he is my Savior. Take time to read this entire psalm that is recorded in 2 Samuel 22. Read it over and over. It is a psalm about the greatness of God in the face of overwhelming difficulty in trouble.

Morning Prayer

God, strengthen the people who are caring for me.

I don't know which is worse. Is it worse to be terminally ill or worse to watch someone you love who is terminally ill? Sometimes I think it is worse to watch someone you love struggle with their own mortality. You feel so helpless. What do you say? What do you do? How do you respond? These are questions for which there are no easy answers. In addition, you have the responsibility of caring for the person who is ill as well as caring for everyone else in your family. You pay the bills. You take care of the kids. You fix whatever is broken in the house. You run back and forth to the hospital. You feel like a juggler with too many balls in the air. And you want to spend as much time as possible with the person who is ill. There aren't enough hours in the day to do everything you need to do. And if there were, you wouldn't have the strength to do it.

It is hard to watch someone work that hard. You wish there was something you could do, but your disease prohibits you from helping. You wish there was something you could say, but whatever you say does not change the reality of the situation. You wish the disease would go away because of what it is doing to your family, but there is nothing you can do to change the situation. You can only pray, "God, give strength to the person who is caring for me."

So who takes care of the caregivers? Usually no one. They grind it out day after day and week after week. It's not like they can take a time-out. There are no time-outs when someone you love is terminally ill. You realize that you have only a limited amount of time, and you wish to spend as much of it as possible with the ill person. You figure that when he or she is gone, you will not regret having spent so much time with your loved one. And you're right.

So who takes care of the caregivers? The only answer I can come up with is God. So I pray for my wife, "God, give her strength to get through today." I have discovered that in our journey together God gives strength each day for all the tasks that need to be done. Usually there is no strength left over; he gives just enough for that day. Remember the words of Paul: "I can do everything through him who gives me strength" (Philippians 4:13).

Evening Promise
We will be like him.

How great is the love the Father has lavished on us, that we should be called children of God! And that is what we are! The reason the world does not know us is that it did not know him. Dear friends, now we are the children of God, and what we will be has not yet been made known. But we know that when he appears, we shall be like him, for we shall see him as he is. (1 John 3:1–2)

Lavish is an interesting word. When we lavish Christmas presents on our children, it means that we have gone overboard.

When we lavish a birthday gift on our spouse, it means that we have gone overboard. And when we talk about the love that the Father has lavished on us, it means that God has gone overboard. And that's exactly what God does. We are his children, and he loves us with an everlasting and unconditional love. His love is not only lavished on us in the present, but it is lavished on us in the future as well.

"What we will be has not yet been made known." What a true statement. While we are assured of heaven and eternity, there is much about heaven and eternity that is beyond our knowledge and understanding. What we do know, however, is that "when [Christ] appears, we shall be like him." Some people interpret this to mean that when we get to heaven, we will all be thirty-three years old just like Jesus. For some people this is a very exciting prospect. When you are sixty or seventy, being thirty-three sounds wonderful. But when you are fifteen or twenty, being thirty-three sounds like you are already over the hill.

So how old will we be in heaven? My wife was three years old when her father passed away. She is now much older than her father was when he passed away. So will she be older than her father in heaven? And what about babies? We know that when they die, they enter into the presence of our Lord. If I lose a baby in this life, will that baby still be a baby when I get to heaven? Or will the baby be a grown adult? And if he is a grown adult, how will I recognize him? And what about my current body? It has been ravaged by the consequences of sickness and disease. Will it look like that when I get to heaven? Let me answer all of these questions: I don't know! All I know is that we will have a body like Jesus Christ. It will be a resurrected body free from all the ravages of sickness and disease, and it will be suited for eternity. I don't know what it will look like or how old it will be, but I know that it will be a reality. And I know that we will recognize everyone else in heaven as well.

God has lavished his love on his children. He has gone overboard. And because he loves us, one day we will be with him. And when we are with him, we will be like Jesus—whatever that means! And whatever it means, it's good enough for me.

Morning Prayer

God, give me faith to believe that you can heal me.

I don't need faith to believe that God can heal; I know God can heal. The Bible is filled with accounts of his power to intervene in sickness and reverse it. I have also known him to heal people during my lifetime. I've known people who were given a few months to live, and God intervened in a miraculous way and healed them. They are living testimonies to the fact that doctors do not have the last word—only God has the last word. So I know that God can heal. And I have the faith to believe that it is within his power to do it. But I need faith to believe that God can heal *me*. There is a huge difference between knowing he can heal others and believing that he can heal me.

It took me a long time to ask God for healing. I'm not sure why. I think I was afraid that he might not heal me. If I went around declaring that I had asked God for healing and God didn't do it, that would be a bad reflection on my prayers. People would think that I did not have enough faith. But one day I was reading in the Bible and came across this text: "You do not have, because you do not ask God" (James 4:2). Then I realized the foolishness of not asking God for healing. So I prayed, "God, give me faith to believe that you can heal me."

What does it mean to have faith to believe that God can heal you? Does it mean that you should no longer have faith in doctors or medicine? I don't think so. I continue to see the doctors and follow their advice even though there is little they can do for my disease. Faith in the Hebrew Scriptures embraces the idea of persistence. So I have decided to keep on believing for healing until God shows me irrefutable evidence that he has something else in mind. For me faith is not so much a moment in time when I have believed God for healing, but rather a consistent belief over time that God is in the process of healing me.

Another way of looking at faith is with the idea of orientation. To believe in Christ for salvation is to be oriented toward Christ. To believe God for healing is to be oriented toward God for healing. My ultimate hope is not in doctors or medicine. My ultimate hope is in the Lord. I'm oriented toward him.

Evening Promise
We all have a Goliath to fight.

"You come against me with sword and spear and javelin, but I come against you in the name of the LORD Almighty, the God of the armies of Israel, whom you have defied." (1 Samuel 17:45)

The story of David and Goliath is one of my favorite stories in the whole Bible. I remember listening to the story in Sunday school and watching the teacher place the various figures on the flannelgraph board. I think this story appeals to kids in a remarkable way because it's about the underdog overcoming incredible obstacles — David, a young shepherd boy, killing Goliath, a giant warrior. We all identify with David because we all have obstacles to overcome in our lives. One of the greatest obstacles is a serious illness or a terminal disease.

According to Scripture, Goliath was over nine feet tall. His armor weighed more than 125 pounds. He was an intimidating figure, and he defied the armies of Israel to send out a man to fight him. When David arrived at the scene, he said, "What will be done for the man who kills this Philistine and removes this disgrace from Israel? Who is this uncircumcised Philistine that he should defy the armies of the living God?" (1 Samuel 17:26). This is the first time in the biblical record that David speaks, and his words are God-focused. David understood that the ultimate battle was not between Goliath and another man, but between Goliath and God.

In this story David actually had to overcome three "Goliaths" in order to have victory. First, he had to overcome the cynicism of his brother. He said to David, "I know how conceited you are and how wicked your heart is; you came down only to watch the battle" (v. 28). Then David had to overcome the advice of Saul. Saul wanted David to put on his own armor to fight Goliath. But David quickly figured out that the armor didn't fit. Finally, he had to fight Goliath himself. Sometimes we have to overcome the cynicism of our own family when we are fighting a disease. Sometimes we have to overcome the advice of those who are experts—doctors. And then we have to stare the disease square in the face and confront it.

David went to the brook and chose five smooth stones and then confronted Goliath with a slingshot in the name of his God. David said, "You come against me with sword and spear and javelin, but I come against you in the name of the LORD Almighty, the God of the armies of Israel, whom you have defied." David understood that he was not fighting Goliath in his own power or strength. Rather, the God who had delivered him from the bear and the lion would also deliver him from Goliath. David understood that the fight was ultimately in God's hands.

So is my fight. While I appreciate the encouragement of family and the advice of doctors, I know that ultimately my medical condition is in the hands of the Great Physician. The odds may be overwhelming. The giant may be over nine feet tall. He may be carrying armor over 125 pounds. But one small stone from God can utterly destroy the giant. This is my hope. One word from God and all of the effects of this disease can be reversed. But even if he chooses not to speak the word, I will still love and trust him. He is still the God who slays giants.

9 780310 463030